# Dancing in the Dark

# Dancing in the Dark

## Reflections on the Problem of Theodicy

## Eric Carlton

Madison • Teaneck
Fairleigh Dickinson University Press

Dancing in the Dark, Words by Howard Deitz. © 1931 Harms Inc, USA, Chappell Music Ltd, London W6 8BS. Reproduced by permission of International Music Publications Ltd., All Rights Reserved.

Associated University Presses
2010 Eastpark Boulevard
Cranbury, NJ 08512

Library of Congress Cataloging-in-Publication Data

Carlton, Eric.
   Dancing in the dark : reflections on the problem of theodicy / Eric Carlton.
      p.   cm.
   Includes bibliographical references and index.
   ISBN 0-8386-4062-1 (alk. paper)
   1. Theodicy.   2. Good and evil.   3. Free will and determinism.   I. Title.
   BL216.C37   2005
   214—dc22                                                        2004019473

PRINTED IN THE UNITED STATES OF AMERICA

Dancing in the dark,
'til the tune ends.
We're dancing in the dark,
and it soon ends.
We're waltzing in the wonder of why we're here.
Time hurries by, we're here,
and then we're gone.

(A popular song dating from the 1930s
by Arthur Schwartz and Howard Deitz)

# Contents

# Dancing in the Dark

# Part I
## The Problem

It is argued by some that the most difficult issue that all religions face is the problem of revelation—or, at least, some clear and unambiguous revelation. Why do the gods stay hidden? Why do they not show themselves to their devotees—as in some of the colorful epiphanies found in ancient Greek myths—so that there will no longer be any room for doubt and uncertainty? And doesn't it undermine religion that so many "revelations" conflict?

All religions have their foundations in real or assumed "revelations." On a sociological analysis, revelations may seem to have come into being for socioeconomic reasons or because of some critical political hiatus in society, such as an actual or threatened invasion and occupation by a foreign power (NB, the common experience in ancient Israel). Or they may appear in what are seen as times of cultural danger (the rise of modern fundamentalist Islam can certainly be interpreted in these terms). However, the movements themselves will almost invariably justify their existence in apocalyptic terms, the natural outcome of certain special insights that are regarded as supernaturally given to a seer or prophet. In such cases the revelation is necessarily *in*direct; it is mediated via human agencies—albeit specially chosen human agencies, as with the self-proclaimed prophet Mohammed. In certain more extreme cases, the human agents may actually claim to be divine—messiahs or "chosen ones," or maybe their immediate followers, will make this claim for them.

However, it hardly needs to be stressed that the whole idea of revelation begs innumerable questions: Even if we are prepared to entertain such notions, by what criteria are we to assess what is and what is not a trustworthy revelation? How would we know whether if in any given instance it was a "true" revelation? And even if we thought it was, how can we know that we understand it correctly? (NB, the wide variety of "understandings" that exist in all the world's "high" or universal religions).

There are several "answers" to these questions, none of which is entirely satisfactory:

1. There is the somewhat dismissive *subjective certainty* answer, which simply insists that one can "know" inwardly that something is true, even though it cannot be verified empirically. The trouble with this kind of intuitive "knowledge" is that it can vary from person to person. Furthermore, it can be, and has been, used to justify all sorts of bizarre practices from idol worship to snake-handling cults. Indeed, some of the worst excesses of religious fanaticism have followed from the conviction of subjective certainty.

2. There is too the *relevation by results* answer, which is really another form of the injunction, "by their fruits shall ye know them." Here the results of the purported revelation are held to demonstrate its authenticity. But again the problem still exists—though at one remove. It presupposes that we always know what ideas and actions serve the appropriate—good or evil—interests. If we think we know, how can we be sure that a particular course of action will have the correct results? Think of the checkered history of the church. How can the same revelation encourage peaceful evangelism and aggressive (i.e., imposed) "conversion"?

3. A safer option is the *does it accord with tradition?* answer. Religious authorities are liable to ask any claimant to a religious experience whether or not it is in line with conventional teaching. This kind of argument has its own kind of circular logic. *If* the religion is "true," it follows that all further revelations must conform to the tradition in order to qualify as "genuine." If they do not, it is argued that they must be ipso facto spurious. Needless to say, this kind of argument makes two sweeping assumptions, namely (i) that the original tradition is true, and (ii) that the guardians of that tradition know just how to judge all additional revelations. So, for instance, the Church of Rome can accept the revelations of Francis of Assisi, doubt the authenticity of Joan of Arc's "voices" for five hundred years (she became Saint Joan only in 1920), and completely reject the reforming "truths" of Martin Luther and John Calvin. And this is not to mention the difficulties the Church had with an emergent science and with the work of Galileo and Giordano Bruno (whom it saw fit to burn at the stake). Such problems derived from the stubborn insistence of churchmen, who argued that they alone knew what accorded with the original tradition.

There are two further responses to the whole question of revelation that are almost diametrically opposed. The first is the view that revelations should not be wholly explicable in naturalistic terms. The assumption is that any revelation that can be explained is hardly worth having. Revelations have to be perplexing to be convincing. Contrary to this is the assumption that all purported revelations must be "reasonable." But who is to judge? Experience shows that what is considered to be reasonable varies with the occasion and the tradition. Indeed, there are often differences within the *same* tradition. One has only to think of the disputes about miracles that still exist in any one tradition. To which events, or alleged events, can we plausibly apply such a term? Or should we dismiss such notions en-

tirely as being altogether unreasonable? Anyway, if history is anything to go by, reason has never been one of the most notable
attributes of institutional systems—religious or otherwise.

The problem with revelatory systems is that they are susceptible to
further and higher revelations. Acceptance of revelation—even the
idea or the possibility of revelation—presupposes a *will to believe* as a
way of coming to terms with intellectual doubts. Traditions are conflicting and ambiguous, but this cannot discount revelation as a logical
possibility. After all, if divinities did manifest themselves—somewhat
like aliens from outer space—they would certainly evoke feelings of
fear and apprehension, not of love or trust.

Indirectly related to the question of revelation is the most intrac-
table problem of all. It subsumes such issues as religious "proofs"
and the nature of evil. It is known technically as the problem of theodicy (in Greek, theos is god, and dikē is justice) and is almost certainly the greatest single issue that besets both believers and would-
be believers in the exercise of faith. In their confrontation with the
cosmos, they have to face the seemingly unresolvable task of trying
to reconcile the justice of god(s) with the suffering of the world. It
is probably the most formidable deterrent to religious belief, and
has generated many answers—none of them wholly satisfactory.

The physical structure of the world of which we are all a part appears to have certain inherent defects that give rise to suffering and
death. This ineradicable presence of disease on the one hand, and
the natural competitiveness of red-in-tooth-and-claw cruelty on the
other, present the well-intentioned believer with seemingly insur-
mountable intellectual difficulties. Yet many have felt constrained to
try to come to terms with this age-old dilemma.

As we examine these various responses, we may feel that here and
there some theorists have at least an inkling as to a possible "solution." Yet at the outset we must recognize that there are, of course,
those for whom this is not a problem at all—though it may still be a
matter of curiosity. This is essentially a problem for monotheists. It
is hardly a problem for those who are confirmed atheists, and it is
only a qualified problem for polytheists and dualists, all of whom
qualify for an exclusion clause. It is also not a problem for those who
do believe in a divine creator—but not a Special Creation—a view
which may well be held by a certain number of monotheists who see
this as a kind of cosmological escape route. All these views will be
considered in more detail in part II.

Any attempt to reconcile the idea of divine goodness with the exis-

tence of that which we regard as evil must begin with an examination of the terms. Here it is customary to distinguish between natural
evil and moral evil. But before we do so, we should look briefly at
the matter of religious language. There are some theorists, especially those in the Wittgensteinian tradition of linguistic philosophy,
who would invoke the argument that the meaning of terms can only
be determined by the particular contexts in which they are used. (In
biblical studies, for example, one is taught that a text out of context
is a pretext.) There is much cogency in this argument. After all, a
term such as, say, "elasticity" means one thing in economic theory,
and something quite different in relation to foundation wear. But a
thoroughgoing relativism about language simply means that morals
mean whatever we want them to mean in the circumstances in which
we use them. (Ask a child what he does at school, and he is likely to
reply "math and stuff," which is reminiscent of the use of the current all-purpose term "cool".) It is not just a matter of imprecision
or sloppy terminology. There are *implicit* understandings here which
may not, however, have universal acceptance. Should language
therefore have some objectivity?

Language *is* important. And it is a problem when one is trying to
express the indefinable and especially the indescribable. Read any
account on an orchestral concert where the critic is trying to tell us
what the music/performance was like (a particular weakness of jazz
critics), and the whole enterprise ends in failure. So if A, how much
more B? If what pertains to the divine is infinitely inexpressible,
what forms of language can possibly be used? And, what is perhaps
more to the point, what forms can possibly make sense?

This issue has been debated at least since the time of Thomas
Aquinas, who argued that such language could not have a strict, literal truth. Gods are not objects of space and time, so how can we
seriously think we can apply to them the sorts of terms that apply to
finite creatures? So when people speak of gods "loving," "speaking," "chastising," or whatever, can the words really have any meaning? The same question applies even more so when we speak of
omniscience and omnipresence. Therefore, when believers talk of
"Allah the merciful" or of Jahweh's "loving kindness," in what sense
does this accord with the facts? Such statements sound like factual
assertions, but where, ask critics, is the evidence? When the sum
total of the world's sufferings are taken into consideration, believers
are stumped for any adequate answer; they have recourse to the argument that human terms do not mean what they appear to mean,

and that the ways of the gods are not our ways. In the end, these seemingly factual assertions become so unclear that "they die the death of a thousand qualifications" (Flew and MacIntyre 1955, 97).

This problem has sometimes been rationalized by insisting that religious language is simply a "model." Theologian Colin Brown seems merely to be reiterating Aquinas when he writes of that which symbolizes truth but is not—and cannot be—truth itself (1969, 176–81). We can only deal in images, signs, and analogies. This, of course, is beyond contention. But, as C. S. Lewis has pointed out, these can only make sense if they represent real things. If we are assured that "God is Love," then it can be presumed that if it means anything at all, it has to mean "love" in something like our sense of the term. Otherwise it has no resonance whatsoever. So if there is truth in this statement, and "Good" and "Evil" are not meaningless terms, then the problem of theodicy remains.

Much of the debate about religious language stems from the work of Ludwig Wittgenstein. He writes of specific "language games," of which religious discourse is one and scientific discourse another. It is a mistake, therefore, to confuse one with another (what philosopher Gilbert Ryle called "category mistakes"). Categories and concepts cannot simply be transferred; to do so merely adds to problems of understanding. Any language game is a "form of life," i.e., part of the cultural milieu and traditions to which it belongs or from which it is derived. Thus, so it is argued, scientific propositions and religious statements, being different universes of discourse, make nonsense to the uninitiated. Each form of life thus becomes self-authenticating; each is its own justification. Hence Ernest Gellner's implied criticism that here we have another validation for a thoroughgoing relativism (1992), and Roger Trigg's comment that to dub something a "form of life" is to protect it from criticism (1975, 66).

Given, however, that our conceptual perspectives, encapsulated in language, help to shape our understanding of the world, do these different paradigms have to mean that cross-fertilization is impossible? Does the scientist who wants to become a believer necessarily have to abandon his scientific viewpoint in order to do so? Is understanding words more important than understanding the world? Words are not inseparable from their underlying meanings. The difficulty with such views is not so much one of purported intelligibility, but the implication that only those on the inside can make the correct judgements about their respective disciplines/communities.

Thus science and religion are not in a position to make valid statements about each other.

In practice, this is patently not the case. In reality, there are few self-contained communities that one can label "scientific people" or "religious people." When one thinks of the wide range of the sciences and scientists, we can see that there is no one "modern high priestly cult . . . of scientists" all linked by their devotion to the "scientific method" (Stanesby 1985, 168). The study of religion can certainly not be classified as a science; indeed, the term "theology" can confidently be regarded as a misnomer. But this does not mean that the study of religious belief and behavior is a waste of time, and it does not preclude the possibility that both religion and science can be combined in rational discourse.

A modern critic within the same language-conscious tradition, Dr. D. Z. Phillips, whose work can often be frustratingly obscure (see 1993b), also endorses the view that any theoretical knowledge or understanding of the divine is just not possible. Anyone, therefore, who denies the existence of the divine is merely rejecting a particular mode of discourse. Religion can only be described and cannot be evaluated objectively. (Phillips's position is rather reminiscent of A. J. Ayer's concerning ethical statements. Ayer saw moral propositions as "meaningless" in a special sense of the term. In effect, he argues that debates about moral values are "meaningless" because they are subjective and consequently do not permit objective validation.) For Phillips, consequently, religion has a kind of psychological adequacy. It is not about belief in a transcendent supernatural power or powers but is simply a way of dealing with the vicissitudes of life.

We can say, therefore, that for Phillips the problem of theodicy (together with that of evil, revelation, and so forth) is a non-issue and thus meaningless as a subject of intelligent discourse. But no matter how one tries to avoid it—and we shall see that many theorists do—the problem will just not go away. And either explicitly or implicitly it still remains the most difficult unsolved religious issue and the greatest obstacle to religious belief.

We can conclude, then, that the divine is not a direct object of experience. But can the divine even be known indirectly, say by inferences from experience? This is confidently asserted by many believers, but such experiences have never been subject to empirical validation. (After all, the divine does not presumably possess those elusive qualities of subatomic particles which, though never seen, are nevertheless detectable in terms of mass and energy and can therefore be expressed in mathematical terms.) No experimental procedure can "reveal" a supraempirical world, regardless of attempts to do so (Carlton 2000). Nor can any unambiguous trace of divine activity be detected in the woeful saga we call history. Indeed, to do so seems to some to be little short of blasphemy (see Popper 1966, vol. 2). Whether, as we shall see, there is evidence of a purposive agency in nature which appears to be so indifferent to human need, is a matter we are about to consider. There are so many "dysteleological" factors: wrong turns in natural and human evolution that seem to suggest an anti-providence at work (Hodges 1979, 18).

We must accept, then, that the divine cannot be precisely defined; neither can the divine be correlated in any plausible sense with the humanly experienced world. Theists understandably appeal not just to our knowledge of the empirical world but also insist that the truth will only be finally known when life is over. This, it has to be admitted, is all rather late, and with the best will in the world, leaves the inquirer with a rather bleak outlook. To argue that the sufferings and evils of the present life will be redressed in a future life is optimistic at best. Such post-mortal verification cannot be known to be true. To the critic, this is mere speculation and has no cognitive value. To the theist, on the other hand, the divine is the Absolute and, being incommensurable, is not to be regarded as an object of speculation. But is this faith of fatalism?

# 1

# Natural Evil

SOME YEARS BEFORE THE ONSET OF HIS CRIPPLING ILLNESS, LSE (LONDON School of Economics) and Cambridge academic Ernest Gellner wrote, "The universe is a torturer, it deprives one of hope but does not allow for assured despair" (1957). There we have the cry—one might also say the anguish—of the concerned agnostic. An intellectual who looks out on our unheeding cosmos which he sees as cruel but perhaps not entirely meaningless. Other philosophers have echoed similar sentiments. In Bertrand Russell one almost detects a poignancy—a kind of wistfulness—when he remonstrates with those who deride philosophy as pointless. He says these may be the views of a scientist or a historian, but hardly the retort of those facing "the prospect of cosmic loneliness" (Russell 1948). It is almost as though Russell was saying, "If only things were different."

Despite all the impressive advances in science, the cosmos is incomprehensible. We are still unable to answer what might appear to be the most elementary questions. How it all began has given rise to much learned speculation, spawning such books as Steven Weinberg's *The First Three Minutes*. Even cosmologists tend to outlaw such questions as "What came before the Big Bang?" and "What caused the Big Bang?"—and certainly not "*Why* was there a Big Bang?" Not even astronomer Sir Martin Rees, in his book with the rather misleading title *Before the Beginning*, purports to tell us. Any "answers" to such questions can only be a form of presumption. Because before the totally mysterious and awesome inception of the cosmos, time as we understand it did not exist. Therefore, from a scientific point of view, such questions are completely meaningless.

Informed scientific opinion has it that we are the product of exploding stars, yet we are only dimly aware of such supernovae. They are usually so far away that they come and go in clusters that are so distant from our own system that they are even unnoticed by astronomers. The most famous event of this kind in what for us is remembered history was noted by the Chinese during the Chih-Ho reign. The "Chief Computer of the Calendar" is said to have reported to the emperor the appearance of a "guest star." No doubt this was interpreted by the Chinese scholar as a propitious omen; otherwise he may well have been soon giving way to his successor.

This was 4 July 1054, and now, a thousand years later, we can see the debris from this cosmic cataclysm in what since 1848 has been known as the Crab Nebula. The explosion actually occurred, of course, in the remote past, its light travelling at three hundred thousand kilometers a second to reach Earth in what we vaguely call the Middle Ages. Its light will continue with us for a long while yet, but what is left is a small neutron star (spinning so fast that it gives off thirty pulses a second) surrounded by filamentary dust which probably represents the constitutive materials for further stars.

The most notable recent supernova was observed by an astronomer in Chile in 1987. It was part of the Large Megellanic Cloud, a kind of mini-galaxy which is nearer to us than our "true" closest galactic neighbor, the Andromeda Galaxy, (M31), which is somewhat over two million light years away. Incidentally, Andromeda, which is one of our local group of twenty or so galaxies, is moving toward us at an incredible rate of one hundred kilometers a second. It is due to join—or collide—with us in about five billion years, just about the time our sun is predicted finally to peter out. (At this point one might dare to repeat the story of the woman who accosted an astromer after a lecture on the solar system to confirm if he had actually said "five billion." "Thank goodness," she said, "for the moment I thought you said 'five million.'")

It is all very well to be told that we are "stardust" (or nuclear waste) left over from supernovae in the depths of space aeons ago, but what kind of assurance is this? How comforting is it to know that we exist, apparently by accident, because of some fearful explosion somewhere in the galaxy in the very remote past? Cosmologists are right to tell us that we can in no way regard ourselves as privileged creatures. The pre-Copernican view that humans were a special creation occupying the center of the universe is now long outdated. Our solar system occupies a tiny niche in the outer reaches of a galaxy containing a hundred thousand million suns—modest by cosmic standards. As Steven Weinberg bluntly put it, in a TV interview, "One thing is for sure, the Earth wasn't made for us."

Yet we can still marvel at the fact that the material components which we comprise, such as carbon, hydrogen, oxygen, etc., coalesced to generate the multiplicity of life forms we find on our planet. Whether these came about spontaneously in some primeval broth—highly unlikely according to some more outré theorists—or whether some life spores found their way to Earth from outer space, is a tantalizing question. This panspermia thesis first advocated in modern times by the Swedish chemist Svante Arrhenius, and more recently popularized by Nobel Prize–winner Francis Crick and astronomer Sir Fred Hoyle, comes in different versions. The most elementary suggests that a comet or asteroid containing self-replicating cells (but from where?) fortuitously landed on the planet, where they found conditions conducive to their development. The more intriguing scenario is that the Earth was deliberately "seeded" by some alien intelligence (in some ways another version of the old Creationist hypothesis), a fascinating idea for which there is, needless to say, no evidence whatsoever. It is an intriguing theory, but it merely replaces one great mystery with another.

Scientists are generally agreed that the Earth and its companion planets began to form from material cast off from the solar nebula between four and five billion years ago. This is relatively young by cosmic standards, given that the universe is estimated to be somewhere between ten and twenty billion years old. The early life of the Earth is thought to have been inconceivably tumultuous. Bombardment from cosmic debris in the form of comets and meteors is believed to have continued for several million years, during which time the Moon also formed, possibly as the result of a cataclysmic impact with another planet-sized body. The thin layer over the Earth's molten core was convulsed by volcanic eruptions, emitting lava and poisonous gases, all of which made the evolution of life quite impossible. So, according to the best estimates, it was not until about 3.5 billion years ago, or perhaps a little earlier, that things settled down, the climage changed, and the first single-celled organisms began to appear.

If the Creationist hypothesis is to be sustained, it begs the question, why by this method? Impressionistically, this seems to be an unncessarily involved and lengthy—not to say uncertain—process for creating a future habitable world. Indeed, the whole affair strikes one as being almost bizarre, especially as we are still living precariously on the wafer-thin crust of a revolving body with a vast molten core.

Whether this was a singular occurrence, we have no way of knowing. Was it, is it, a one-off phenomenon? Or can we reasonably hypothesize that given similar climatic conditions and the right mix of essential minerals, life—as we understand the term—was actually inevitable? Some theorists (e.g., Monod [1971] 1972) have argued that life on Earth, though consistent with natural laws, is a unique phenomenon. They concede that its origination was an extremely improbable event, and could only have taken place because of a highly complex sequence of apparently random stages. (It was the extreme unlikelihood of such an event that contributed to the generation of the panspermia hypothesis.) But the doctors differ. Some seem to be almost ideologically committed to the unique-event view, while others even insist that the whole process will one day be reproduced in a laboratory, although experiments so far have been singularly unsuccessful. Life from non-life, both little-understood terms, is still, as yet, an unfathomable mystery.

Another perplexing problem for those who believe—or want to believe—that the planet was divinely created for human beings is the history of mass extinctions. It is now no longer mere speculation that in the distant past the wholesale destruction of entire species has taken place. By some estimates, ninety-nine percent of all the species that ever lived have since vanished. Research appears to have confirmed, by various techniques of chemical and geological analysis, that this happened at least five times, the most serious of which took place in the Triassic period some 245 million years ago for reasons that are as yet uncertain. There may have been a drastic change in climate (extreme drought, freezing temperatures, volcanic eruptions and extensive floods still wreak havoc, as we know only too well), or there may have been a build-up of carbon dioxide which poisoned the oceans, as some researchers believe. On the other hand, devastation may have had an extraterrestrial source. It is now generally accepted by scientists that the impact of an asteroid or comet many miles in diameter brought about the extinction of the dinosaurs and other species during the Cretaceous period sixty-five million years ago. Ratification seems to have come from the discovery of a one-hundred-mile-diameter crater in the Yucatán Peninsula in Mexico, which can be dated to this period.

This all begs the supplementary question, why dinosaurs? The fossil evidence indicates that the dinosaur age lasted for about 140 million years, i.e., culminating in circa sixty-five million BC. Why did such creatures dominate the Earth for such an incredibly long period? From a Creationist point of view, this makes no sense at all. Unless, of course, it is argued that the dinosaurs were deliberately destroyed by divine intervention in order to make way for other species and ultimately for human beings. But only a moment's thought will show what a fallacious argument this is. It means that this and the occurrence of all the other mass extinctions were a series of false starts, and that the creator(s) didn't really know what they were about. It bears some similarity in its implications to the literal acceptance of the Hebrew Flood story (almost certainly drawn originally from ancient Mesopotamian sources). Here again, god (El) is depicted as having "regretted that he ever made man." In other words, El was having second thoughts. The irony then is that El makes yet a further miscalculation. Now, having destroyed the human race, except for Noah and his family, El allows this favored remnant to reproduce and repopulate the Earth, whereupon it becomes, if anything, worse than it was before.

So rather than the false-start hypothesis of divine creation, is it better and more persuasive not to begin at this point at all? And yet creation has got to start somewhere, and the consensus view of science—that we must begin with a tiny ball of infinitely compressed energy which had the potential to form a cosmos of immeasurable dimensions and inconceivable complexity—defies the imagination and itself requires an act of faith. Whether we must choose between an eternal creation or an eternal creator is a moot point. Perhaps the two conceptions may yet be reconciled.

Perhaps what we tend to overlook in the modern world is the fact that the idea of a special creation is a feature of the High (universal) religions and that they all originated and developed in a prescientific era. They are all characterized by a geocentricism which inevitably limited their conception of what the cosmos could possibly be. A few perceptive—one might almost say daring—spirits in the ancient world such as Democritus and later Heraclitus ventured to suggest otherwise, but most people preferred to believe the evidence of their senses. The Earth looked flat, the Sun seemed to go round the Earth, so ipso facto, the Earth was the center of the universe. It was a privileged place which the divinities had created specially for human beings. Everything is provided, either actually or potentially, for our benefit. As the Hebrew scriptures make clear, the Earth and ultimately humans are the crown of the Creation. (No one was surely ever meant to take this account literally. Yet even in this poetic scenario there are hints of the true reality. We are told that "The Earth was originally without form and void"; and the depiction of the paradisal environment of the Garden of Eden, and its creatures, are clearly couched in symbolic terms, while its humans' "Fall" is transparently an instructive morality tale.)

But now that we know—or should know—that this is not the case, such ideas are retained vestigially and implicitly in modified forms. Some creationists do still exist even among educated people, notably those who belong to some type of fundamentalist religious organization. They will give a reluctant deferential nod in the direction of science and admit that the Earth and its creatures were specially created though an evolutionary process. (Though I once interviewed a young minister of religion who insisted that he "repudiated evolution.") Neo-creationists argue that they do not have to believe in a divine Magician who, ex nihilo, is able to produce the universe out of his cosmic hat. A slow but deliberate process of evolution will do just as well. But the impression is unavoidable that very many would-be believers suffer from some form of cognitive dissonance. They are trying to hold two apparently contradictory sets of beliefs at the same time. How they try to reconcile these beliefs is the subject of the ensuing discussion.

These concessions to science are not without their problems. There are still arguments and uncertainties in the "trade" about evolution, but there is a general consensus among scientists that Charles Darwin's line of reasoning is correct. There is still much that is unexplained, especially about the actual stages of development and the puzzle of species morphology (are birds really descended from dinosaurs?), but still the overall thesis of selection and adaptation is now regarded as incontravertible. Yet, as we have already noted, the question of how life can have arisen from non-life remains one of science's great unsolved mysteries.

Discounting the plausible though not generally accepted panspermia thesis which has a certain appeal for neo-creationists, most researchers opt for a synthesis of relatively simple organic molecules which then spontaneously generated a protective membrane and inexplicably developed the capacity for self-replication. It is assumed that this came about by metabolizing outside energy. Hypothetically, all this happened in one or more primordial pools or oceans, possibly assisted by catalytic electrical charges, presumably from lightening. Underlying such assumptions there lies the further mystery of the cells themselves. Science is even now still trying to unravel the wonder of their incredible complexity, and how they contain the genetic codes that are common to all living things.

Yet in uncovering these biological complexities, researchers point to the wastefulness and inefficiencies of the evolutionary process. Life forms are complex competitive systems which sometimes evolve in strange, non-rational ways. The constant struggle for survival has the luxury of time, but this does not mean that there are no evolutionary dead ends. Every so often—and perhaps more often than even the specialists appreciate—there have been inexplicable mutations. These have sometimes been beneficial, but at other times have resulted in false starts in the evolutionary process. Some biologists have made a point of citing "the many apparently silly inefficiencies of living systems—vestigial organs, junk DNA, the odd position of light-sensing cells in the human eye" (Hazen 1997, 169), all of which support the view that life as we know it has certainly evolved from simpler forms and has been a somewhat haphazard affair.

However, in general, the systems work well. Regardless of the enormous strides that have been made in modern science, researchers are still at a loss to explain exactly how such a vast amount of information can be stored, duplicated, and interpreted in something as tiny as a living cell. Every human being has about eighty thousand genes that carry the coded information. Researchers are now involved in the monumental task of identifying these genes and the structures and function of their associated proteins. And this is not all. Determining the complete structure of a protein molecule can take a research team years to complete. We know a great deal about the mechanisms, but precisely how they work is still a problem. How is the genetic information coded in DNA converted into the actual constituents of living creatures? We know the agents, but what about the process? This is a trick we have yet to learn.

We now know that minute changes in the genetic code can produce random variations which can have a dramatic effect on the organism. Just one error (i.e., one genetic "letter" out of billions in the alphabetic sequence) can result in a competitive advantage or in an evolutionary dead end. Not unusually it can result in a mutational disaster such as a hereditary disease which may be impossible to eradicate. There are all too many such diseases. Some three thousand or so have already been identified, and each can be attributed to a particular gene defect (the debilitating condition known as sickle-cell anemia, so common in the developing world, is a case in point). It is to be fervently hoped that the Human Genome Project will supply some of the answers we need to prevent or even cure such diseases, at least in particular cases. The defects in the genetic information that cause such diseases as cystic fibrosis, muscular dystrophy, and certain hereditary forms of cancer are now reasonably well understood at the molecular level, but problems still remain concerning the "repair" of genetic material. Similarly, attempts to thwart the AIDS virus are still eluding the massive efforts of medical researchers, particularly in their endeavor to prime patients' immune systems so as to counter the infection.

What is abundantly clear to those with only a rudimentary knowledge of biology is that life has developed by means of a complex evolutionary process. But why like this? If the Creation is purposeful, why employ this bewildering array of finely-tuned mechanisms that have taken at least 3.5 billion years to reach the present stage? And is evolution "finished"? Are humans the apogee of creation, or is there something more to come? Homo sapiens has been around for less than a million years and what we ambitiously call "civilization" for a mere six thousand years, which is as yesterday on a cosmic scale. Of course, it can always be argued that the gods are in no hurry. But the aeons found necessary for the appearance of the human animal does seem a bit excessive.

A supplementary question that must be asked is what was the point of all those prehuman humans who preceded Homo sapiens? Were these evolutionary failures? This has to be the conclusion of those who regard modern humans as a special creation. They will concede a prehuman stage but insist that the process was discontinuous and that there was a definite, divinely ordained break between these primitive prehumans and ourselves. But then why the prehumans? (I'm reminded of that marvellous cartoon—difficult to reproduce in words—of a shaggy Neanderthal family, the father of which is talking to a sharply attired salesman and saying, "there's no doubt about it, Sid, evolution's been good to you.")

The process of evolution, then, though incredibly ingenious, is long and laborious, and it doesn't seem to make sense to have a series of involved preparatory stages leading to a special creation of human beings. Monsters and mishaps have occurred that appear to have served no particular purpose. To complicate the issue still further, we know that at the nonhuman level, evolution is still taking place. The medical world, for instance, is anxious that bacteria are developing resistant strains to antibiotics, almost as though there was a kind of mindless conspiracy afoot to ensure that we humans are kept in our place.

Creationists also have to face the further difficulty of trying to explain the amazing yet disturbing diversity of life on the planet. Why do certain creatures exist? (I was recently involved in a conversation that went something like this:

"What are lacewings for?"

"They are there to eat aphids."

"Well, what are aphids for?"

"Oh, they are there for lacewings to eat."

It's the kind of circular argument that leaves one wondering whether the natural world could therefore do without both lacewings and aphids).

One hardly needs to reiterate the fact that nature is "red in tooth and claw." Dig up any square meter of earth in the garden, and one can see nature in action. Little creatures are in the act of devouring or being devoured. This goes for the larger world as well in the process we dispassionately refer to as the "food chain." Mother Nature—surely a misnomer—has a strange yet coldly efficient way of caring for her children. This is how evolution works, by eliminating the weak and facilitating the survival of those best adapted to their environments. (Wasn't it Adolf Hitler, intent on aggressive war in the East, who said that "nature knows nothing of clemency . . ."?) There are, of course, exceptions—but these are anomalies.

There was a time, as we well know, when the whole idea of evolution was contested, mainly on religious grounds, and Darwinian advocate Thomas Huxley had to remind critics that they intrude in areas outside their professional competence. But it is interesting to ask *why* these clerics indulged, as Huxley put it, in "aimless rhetoric [and] . . . eloquent digressions and skilled appeals to religious prejudice." Huxley's retort to Bishop Wilberforce in a famous debate in 1860 is quoted by Robert Hazen (1997, 197), who likewise doesn't ask this question. Clerics like Wilberforce were not just concerned about the "monkey-to-man" issue; they were at a loss to know why the Creator should work in this way. As a theory, evolution seemed not only to undermine the dignity of human nature, it was also an affront to the divine order of things. It defied what many religious people like to call "consecrated common sense."

But we cannot deny the facts. In a highly generalized sense, the theory of evolution works. We are well aware of the fact that various creatures, including humans, display the vestigial characteristics of earlier forms. And biologists are able to trace and document the subtle changes in living things as an ongoing process. But if the Creationist hypothesis that our world was made for us has any validity, why such a variety of forms, and why such bizarre and predatory creatures? And why so many that obviously serve no useful purpose other than to prey upon and to be preyed upon by other life forms? And, not least, why all this extravagant evolutionary activity in a world that is always hanging by a thread, anyway? We could all be due for another ice age, an asteroid impact, or some other form of extinction either from natural causes or our own ignorance and stupidity.

About eleven thousand years ago, North and South America lost roughly two-thirds of their large mammal population, possibly due to a combination of natural and human agencies. The fossil evidence suggests that fifty thousand years ago Australia had possibly fifty species of large mammals; now it has only four. Hawaii has lost over half of its native bird population, and many other exotic creatures have been hunted to extinction. Some ecologists believe that the planet is losing some of its more obscure species at the rate of several per day. Again this is partly due to natural causes and partly due to the unstemmed growth of the human population, which, among other things, brings soil erosion and the depletion of necessary nutrients that damage the ecosystem.

Ecologists such as Paul Erlich deplore—perhaps rightly—such a state of affairs. Maybe we do have a duty to our only known living companions in the universe. And perhaps we are doing irrevocable damage to the environment. This is part of the rarely contested wisdom of environmental science. But is this simply a case of a punctuated equilibrium? Will nature—as always (?)—restore another kind of balance? And doesn't progress—whatever that means—involve controlling and changing the environment to accommodate human needs?

## MICRO NATURAL EVIL

So does nature really know best, or can we do without some of these species that appear to have no very useful—indeed, providential—purpose? (We must all have wondered about the ubiquitous presence of such things as lice and flies.) At a basic, and most disturbing, level we might consider the microbes and parasites with which the world is infested. These must certainly rank among the most unwanted denizens of the planet, and their effects must come very high on the list of those things we class as natural evil.

We are surrounded all the time by millions of tiny but potent microbes that are eager to invade our bodies and occupy our organs and tissues. The most insidious is surely the virus which must find a host body eventually or die. Viruses must be among the most successful of all life forms, invading unwilling cells and multiplying usually to the detriment of the host. They do this by changing the cell's genetic instructions and producing their own program for replication. They then burst out of the dying cell's protective membrane and invade others in order to continue the process.

Very few antiviral agents have so far been developed. The medical profession has, as yet, very limited remedies to offer, although some specific vaccines are available. Sometimes the host's immune system is able to neutralize the virus's worst effects, but often this just does not work. So, for instance, a Herpes Simplex virus (the kind that produces the common cold sore) will stay in the body indefinitely. While another form of the herpes virus (Type 2), which causes what is generally known as genital herpes and is very much on the increase, has still not responded successfully to antiviral agents. Once entrenched in the nerve cells, it too may never leave the host system. It is simply reactivated on an irregular basis as the opportunity occurs—a painful condition which is there for life. In yet a further form (Herpes Zoster), it causes chicken pox in childhood and may reappear as shingles in later life.

A virus (literally a "poison that disturbs the spirit") is infinitesimally small, often no more than a few nanometers long (a nanometer is one millionth of a meter). As one specialist has suggested, just a single drop of blood from a pinprick will contain something like five million red blood cells, each of which could house thousands of viruses (Dwyer 1989). Although viruses need a host for their long-term existence, they can live outside the body by forming a protein-based protective coating known as a capsid. And what is particularly insidious is that viruses are adapted to connect with certain receptors on the surface of the body's cells. Thus they become disease-specific, so that, say, influenza viruses do not encroach upon the preserves of the herpes viruses.

Plants, animals, insects, and even bacteria can be affected by viruses. As humans we are constantly at risk from infection in very many ways; indeed, it's something of a wonder that we are as reasonably healthy as we are. But when a virus does strike, most notably among the most vulnerable, it can be devastating (e.g., German measles to fetuses and very young children, and influenza among the old and those weakened by malnutrition). Most treacherous of all are those viruses that have "learned" how not only to infect the cell but have also developed the capactity to kill the resistant cells of the immune system, as is the case with AIDS (Acquired Immunodeficiency Syndrome), which is now possibly the most terrible viral menace in the modern world.

However, by way of illustration, let us begin with influenza. Of all the large-scale epidemics (or perhaps, better still, pandemics) few have wrought more havoc than influenza. Today, with the advent of antibiotics, its effects have been largely neutralized (although note the way in which many people are inclined to upgrade their symptoms from a cold to a "touch of flu"). But this was not always the case, and still isn't when periodically a new strain of the influenza virus hits the West (Spanish flu, Asian flu, Hong Kong flu, etc.).

The ravages of influenza go back some way and have been so widespread that some delimitation is required. So we will concentrate on Europe. There were outbreaks in the early sixteenth century in Italy, hence the term influenza (or influence), which was thought to be caused by the "astrological effect" of the stars. In the eighteenth century, when the virus was as yet unknown, the disease was still not clearly identified. The symptoms were those many of us know well, and the main recommended treatment was simply bedrest. The disease spread from Italy to France, Belgium, and Germany, but— interestingly—not to Scandinavia. There were relatively few deaths at this time, but with more outbreaks later in the century, the effects were more severe. These may have begun in Russia, and what limited evidence we have suggests that the virus's effects became very widespread, even reaching to the Americas. Most of the victims appear to have been the very young and the elderly. There were further outbreaks throughout the eighteenth century, but morbidity (incidence), though high, brought relatively few deaths. Late in the century, there were major outbreaks of the disease, which this time may have originated in China and which spread to Russia, where it is said that many thousands were affected every day; from there it spread to most of Europe, the Caribbean, and the United States.

There were further significant outbreaks in the nineteenth century, when Germany and Russia were again badly affected. The virus again moved swiftly throughout the Continent and Asia, facilitated no doubt by the improved transport networks which were then being developed for trade and travel. By this time it was taking a more lethal form. In the mid-century outbreak, the Mediterranean area was seriously hit, and in the late-century epidemic (the first to be extensively documented), when it was again found in the Americas and Africa, the effects were more serious still. The disease—if one can confidently call it *one* disease—seems to have been increasing in potency; in Europe alone it is estimated to have caused over three hundred thousand deaths. But it was in the latter part of the century that more detailed studies were being made of the disease, and science was beginning to dispel earlier quite erroneous notions of its cause and how it was contracted. The contagious nature of the disease was now recognized, and attempts were even made to try to isolate the microorganism itself.

However, it was the so-called Spanish influenza epidemic in the aftermath of the First World War that the disease caused unimaginable suffering and death. Between 1917 and 1919 influenza killed more people than the war. It can justly be compared with some of the worst plagues in history. The Black Death caused by bubonic plague in the fourteenth century ravaged Asia and Europe and killed at least twenty-five million Europeans (including perhaps a third of the population of Great Britain). And this was not the first outbreak of bubonic plague caused by a bacillus transmitted by fleas from infected rats. In the sixth century, the Plague of Justinian (ruler of the Eastern Roman Empire) is reputed to have been killing upwards of five thousand people a day in the capital Constantinople (Istanbul) alone. The provenance of bubonic plague is uncertain, but it is believed to have come originally from Africa and India and was then transported on rat-infested ships to Europe.

Where Spanish flu originated is also not certain; it was labelled "Spanish" simply because Spain is where the first serious outbreak occurred. From Spain, where it is estimated to have affected some eight million people, it spread to the European battlefields and proved as lethal as the military hardware. Soon there were outbreaks in Paris and at a number of French seaports. The disease was then transported to the United States, where some Army camps were reporting a death every hour; while in Britain it was soon claiming two thousand lives a week. Medical authorities did what they could in the circumstances, but they were unable either to check the disease or to do much for the sick. Quarantine was tried, but to little avail. Deaths multiplied largely because the disease was not clearly understood, and its unabated spread meant that the emergency services were stretched to the limit, while the toll still continued to rise.

By 1918–19, the disease had become a worldwide epidemic. Poorer countries were particularly badly affected, especially China and, more notably, India, where it is thought that over twelve million people died. What baffled the scientists for some time afterwards was that they were dealing with an unknown radical mutation of the influenza virus that had probably originated in pigs and poultry (common reservoirs for the virus). Indeed, it may have again changed its form before invading the human population, which had no natural immunity to this new genetic scourge. In all, it is estimated that as many as twenty million people died of the virus. Natural evil can be a greater menace than moral evil.

It hardly needs to be emphasised that the most frightening viral infection of our time is HIV/AIDS. It is without question the most lethal of the sexually transmitted diseases (STDs). Many of these have been around since earliest times but increase in incidence and severity under conducive conditions. With the introduction of antibiotics in the 1940s, many people thought that such diseases—most notably syphilis and gonorrhea—were headed for extinction, but these and other resistant forms of STDs are causing specialists to rethink the situation. It is often said that every system brings with it its own evils, and as far as STDs are concerned it is certainly true that new patterns of behavior bring their own evils. And nowhere is this better evidenced than with the phenomenal incidence of HIV/AIDS, especially in the developing world.

The HIV/AIDS virus is transmitted by a process of fluid exchange, which effectively means either by sexual intercourse (both homosexual and heterosexual) or by intravenous injections by drug users and hemophiliacs. And sometimes, by a somewhat bizarre amalgam of both sex and drugs, as with drug users, especially crack cocaine addicts, who exchange sex *for* drugs. The virus, or family of viruses, may well have been around since prehuman times mainly in mammals (there is, for example, a feline Immunodeficiency Virus that affects various members of the cat family), but normally these do not harm humans. The HIV/AIDS virus, however, is a retrovirus somewhat like that which causes T-cell leukemia and probably originated in Central Africa in certain primates. (There is a simian form of the disease that kills certain types of monkeys.) It may possibly have caused some deaths in the West as early as the 1950s, though at that time it was unrecognized. It appeared in Africa in the 1960s and made its debut in the United States in the 1980s, then almost exclusively among homosexual males and drug users who shared needles.

It is now known that there are several types of the virus (as many as thirty have been reported) and that these mutate in order to resist or evade a host's immune defenses. By the time the symptoms appear, the person may actually be harboring several types of the virus—in which case they haven't a chance. The incidence of the disease has been rapidly enhanced by a number of factors: international travel, especially people taking exotic (and erotic) holidays; the greatly increased practice of injecting addictive drugs, most nobably with unsterilized hypodermics; and, not least, homosexual and heterosexual prostitution. Added to these is the critical factor of ignorance and a cavalier indifference to consequences, especially in parts of Africa and Asia where the disease has reached pandemic proportions.

The numbers infected can only be guessed. Probably in sub-Saharan Africa alone, according to the World Health Organization (WHO), at least ten million are affected, principally in Zaire, Zambia, Uganda, Malawi, Rwanda, Kenya, Tanzania, and South Africa. The situation has not been helped by the failure to recognize the disease in many of the states by both the people and the authorities. Often it has been confused with other conditions, especially when the AIDS stage is reached and the complete breakdown of the immune system has allowed other diseases such as TB (tuberculosis) and various cancers to develop. The situation is now so critical, with no certain cure or antidote in sight, that some specialists speculate that the virus may mutate to an airborne form, somewhat like influenza. If this should happen, the prospects are terrifying. The world would be facing another Black Death and the possibility of devastation on a monumental scale (Karlen, 1995, 193).

It is an old adage that if anyone wants to get an infection, the best place to go is a hospital. It is disturbingly simple to succumb to infection, especially in postoperative conditions. Despite all attempts at sanitary thoroughness, this is the place where viruses and bacteria abound. So let us consider bacteria. They are unlike viruses in that they do not need a host in order to survive. Tetanus is a good example. (I recall working as a nursing orderly during my students days and having to care for a man who was critically ill with tetanus, which he apparently contracted while gardening). Tetanus spores can survive in the soil in quite extreme conditions of heat, cold, and drought yet still infect the wounds of the unwary. Like so many other microorganisms such as anthrax and various staphylococci, it has been one of nature's "gifts" since prehuman times.

Bacterial organisms such as those that cause leprosy and TB are also quite at home inside the body's cells. There they can adapt themselves to changing conditions, particularly those created by the introduction of antibiotics. Though without intelligence, they seem to be fiendishly ingenious in adapting to any threat to their existence. What with viruses, fungi, bacteria and sundry microparasites, it would almost appear that nature had conspired to ensure that in the end we humans cannot win. One suspects that if one day human beings in their gross stupidity finally destroy themselves, these persistent little creatures would still be around.

TB is typically one of those diseases that, in the West at least, we thought had been conquered, especially with such antibiotics as streptomycin. But this is not the case. In recent years, possibly with the influx of immigrants from the developing nations, it is now on the increase again. TB, which affects the bones and particularly the lungs, is spread by air droplets and the inhalation of the tubercle bacilli. These come in two types: one is found in domestic animals, made the transition to humans long ago, and can be found in Neolithic and Bronze age skeletons; the other, almost certainly a mutation from the first, is far worse. Often known as consumption or pulmonary tuberculosis, it became widespread in Asia and the Near East, from where it travelled to Greece (the early physician, Hippocrates, described the symptoms in some detail) and from there to Rome. It thrived in the crowded conditions of medieval cities, where it played a complementary role with leprosy, whose bacilli are rather similar and which share a common "disease pool." Both were then somewhat outdone by the Black Death (bubonic plague), and, in one form or another, this deadly triumvirate is still with us.

The tuberculosis bacteria are slowgrowing and infect far more people than they kill. But they can lie dormant for ages and are quite resistant to the human immune system. Once in their contagious stage, they can be highly infectious. One authority gives the example of a schoolgirl in California in 1993 who infected four hundred other pupils (Karlen 1995, 208).

The Industrial Revolution provided ideal conditions of overcrowding and malnutrition in which TB could flourish, and by 1900, the "white plague," as it had become known, killed more people worldwide than any other infection and rivalled malaria as public enemy number one. But by the mid-twentieth century, antibiotics were shown to be so effective that by 1970 much research into TB had all but dried up. Yet there were still a few pessimistic (realistic?) souls who predicted its return in a more resistant form. In 1984—that ominous year—they were proved right.

What is now called MDR tuberculosis has appeared in several strains, some of which are completely untouched by any antibiotics and are now making their presence felt. TB has now increased in the West and alarmingly so in Africa, where it often goes hand-in-glove with HIV/AIDS. It is an opportunistic disease and is always prepared to strike the most vulnerable. It affects over one and a half billion people worldwide, of which about ten million have "active" tuberculosis at any one time, and of these some three million will die each year.

As a killer disease, TB is closely rivalled by malaria in its ability to carry off large swathes of population, especially in the developing world. Like TB, mortality does not equal morbidity, but the figures are, nevertheless, quite horrendous. It is well known that malaria is a parasitic disease carried by the Anopheles mosquito and has been with us since the remote past. It may have originally been introduced to humans by infected birds, but this is still quite uncertain. What we do know is that birds and various kinds of domestic animals have been the unwitting hosts of a number of diseases that have then been passed to humans. As for the mosquito, of which there are very many species, it too has been the vector of some of the worse diseases to infect the planet, including yellow fever and its close relation dengue fever. Both are viral infections, and between them they have accounted for literally innumerable deaths, especially of children. These have mainly been in tropical countries, but not exclusively so. In the early nineteenth century, between eighteen thousand and twenty thousand people died of yellow fever in Barcelona. It was commonly believed to have been imported from the Caribbean and perhaps originally from West Africa, where it is endemic. Also in the nineteenth century, there were very serious outbreaks of dengue fever and yellow fever in the United States, the latter claiming some twenty thousand lives.

One could continue in this vein almost indefinitely. We have not mentioned smallpox, cholera, polio, typhus, meningitis, encephalitis, etc. Nor have we considered the host of new diseases (many of which appear to emanate from tropical rain forests) such as Ebola fever, Lassa fever, the deadly hemorrhagic fevers, Marburg disease, Legionnaires disease, Lyme disease, and so on. Then there are the new—or new to us—venereal diseases such as chlamydia and, of course, HIV/AIDS. It would seem that as soon as one is identified and temporarily checked, another appears.

So why are they here? Can their presence possibly accord with the

Special Creation hypothesis? Take as one more example the pathogen known as the schistosome. This is a microscopic parasite that enters humans from water containing infected snails. Their eggs have been found in Egyptian mummies three thousand years old; even then, as now, they killed in a number of unpleasant ways, including by bladder damage and lesions to the liver and lungs. Today the disease is estimated to infect as many as one hundred million people worldwide.

Parasites, like other creatures, survive at the expense of others. Multicelled parasites such as tapeworms survive by invading their hosts, while others such as ticks tap their victims from without. Viruses thrive on almost anything alive; fungi and bacteria scavenge plants and animals, though in doing so may bring about their own demise. The animals, in turn, browse on the plants, while others— the carnivores, including humans—prey on their fellow animals. It's an endless biological drama.

Is this all necessary? It all seems to be such an ill-thought-out and wasteful system. Admittedly, some microorganisms are beneficial, but do these compensate for the unimaginable harm done by their less-discriminating counterparts? We are surely forced to ask, could not a benevolent and creative mind have invented a more rational and less destructive earthly economy?

## MACRO NATURAL EVIL

In considering the Special Creation hypothesis that is held either explicitly or implicitly by religious believers, we must return to those problems relating to the precariousness of the planet.

First there is the issue of *function*. In the sciences in particular, the term "function" can be applied in a number of different ways. Function for what? Function for whom? There is, too, the important difference between *ideal* function and *actual* function. Furthermore, the use of the term "function" presupposes that we know in advance what we should expect; we make a value judgement, as when we speak, say, of the function of the National Health Service. But what concerns us here is the distinction between function as that which can be anticipated in a given set of conditions, and function in terms of purpose. This distinction has critical biological and cosmological implications. Scientists tend to be very wary of arguments from purpose or what are more technically known as teleological (end-state) statements. Arguments from purpose suggest design—so is there a designer?

Our planet is poised in space in such a way that conditions—to be specified—have given rise to a multitude of life forms. No other planet in our solar system displays these same life-giving or life-enhancing properties. Is this a matter of design, or is it, fortuitously, simply a function of the planet's proximity to the sun? It is just possible that some primitive fungal life forms might exist on some of the moons of the gas giants, Saturn and Jupiter, and even more likely on our near neighbour, Mars, but so far there is no evidence to support such speculations. So, as far as we know, we are alone in the solar system, and some theorists somewhat implausibly hypothesize that we may actually be alone in the universe.

So why us? And if we are so privileged, why is it that our planetary home (that "small blue spot," as Carl Sagan called it) is such a precarious place to be? Why a lopsided lump of molten iron swirling at some sixteen hundred kilometers an hour with a thin habitable crust that is so prone to movement and fissures? And why a planet that has been, and almost certainly still is, vulnerable to cometary activity that could spell extinction? And why is it subject to the critical vagaries of temperature, with ice ages that can last for several thousand years and eliminate all but the most adaptable life forms? In Ernest Zebrowski's words, "Mother Nature chooses barely to whisper her answers to our most compelling questions" (1997, x).

No one of these factors—and certainly not all of them taken together—can possibly support the Special Creation hypothesis. We live on a restless planet, with the hazards of volcanic eruptions/ earthquakes, hurricanes, tornadoes, and tsunamis. Perhaps it is fortunate that there is a disparity between the human life span and the frequency of disasters, otherwise we would each pass away before we had the opportunity to transmit our genetic legacies. Statistically, the chances that any individual will die in a natural disaster are very small, but the chances of such a disaster somewhere that will kill someone are very high. Indeed, they are both frequent and certain.

Considering the way our planet came into being, perhaps we can expect exactly what we have: the original fireball expanding immeasurably; the gradual emergence of the chemical constituents of the cosmos producing the intricate pattern of stars and galaxies that we now see, whose photons of light began their journey billions of years ago; and the solar system as one speck in the outer reaches of an unexceptional spiral galaxy formed from clouds of cosmic dust. On this scale, the Earth seems modest indeed, a mere collocation of common particles which was both fortuitous and fragile. Held in space as it is by its metronomic spin and the gravitational pull of its parent sun, it is little wonder that it is subject to the vortices of climate, winds, atmosphere, and so forth.

We are all, then, under something of an obligation that it finally developed the biosphere it did. But to what extent does this confirm or at least indicate a Special Creation? And how many people have rejected such a hypothesis either because periodic cataclysms seem to belie such a view, or because when they do occur they are attributed to divine disfavor? The philosopher Voltaire reacted against the divine-disfavor argument, which was advanced to account for the terrible Lisbon earthquake in November 1755. In fact, he inveighed against the Church in his satire, *Candide,* where the Inquisitors believe that by punishing those who ascribe such incidents to "natural law," they will avert further disasters. It follows that where organizations such as the Inquisition are set up to extirpate heresy, they are likely to see heresy everywhere.

The Lisbon disaster was one of the worst to affect a major center of population. Hundreds of magnificent buildings were destroyed, crushing and burying thousands of people. The actual death toll is uncertain, but it has been reasonably estimated at about fifty thousand. The initial three shocks were followed by seismic sea waves (tsunamis) some eighty minutes later. Those who had fled to the seafront after the earthquake hit the center of the city were simply swept into oblivion. Needless to say, it was the arrival of these huge waves that caused the most panic. Tsunamis, which may reach heights of 12 meters or more, can pour in water for up to thirty minutes after retreating and taking bodies like mere flotsam with them. It was these that survivors most clearly remembered and which are graphically depicted in contemporary accounts of the disaster.

The earthquake was felt over the entire Iberian Peninsula, and there were even reports of aftershocks as far afield as the North African coast. It is now thought that it would have registered about 8.75 on the Richter scale, which would make it one of the most powerful earthquakes ever recorded. In Richter scale terms it comes close to the earthquake in San Francisco in 1906 (8.2) and Alaska in 1964 (9.3). But the Richter scale doesn't tell us everything. The true severity can only be judged by the death tolls: Antioch in 526 (250,000), Shaanxi, China in 1556 (830,000); Yokohama, Japan in 1923 (200,000); Nan-Shan, China in 1927 (200,000); and Tangshan, also in China, where in 1976 it is estimated that 242,000 people died. And such figures tend to discount those who suffer in the aftermath of such calamities from starvation and disease.

Seismic activity can sometimes be predicted with some accuracy, thus giving inhabitants of the threatened zones some advance warning. But usually only the most general assumptions can be made based upon our limited knowledge of the fault lines in the Earth's crust. The movement of the vast tectonic plates are, as yet, little understood, so that, for example, seismologists can only say that the San Andreas fault in the western United States will produce another earthquake—maybe in fifty years, or maybe next week. There were minor quakes in the San Francisco–Los Angeles area as recently as 1989 and 1994, and experts confidently expect a repeat of the 1906 catastrophe.

Closely allied to earthquakes are the phenomena of volcanic eruptions. These fortunately give rather more warning of impending disaster, but what is unfortunately disguised is the actual severity of the eruption. No one is ever quite sure after the initial showers of ash just how bad things are going to be. Again it is a problem of tectonics. A rising plate will cause the release of molten rock which is then spewed out onto the Earth's surface as lava. Mercifully, really devastating volcanic eruptions are fairly rare, but they do demonstrate unequivocally just how fragile the Earth's crust really is.

Rare or not, the problem is a perennial one. Scientists are quite certain that some volcanoes remain potentially active for up to ten million years. But because volcanic activity is unusual, in certain areas (e.g., Italy and Sicily) people will insist on setting up home in danger zones (compare how villagers in such places as Bangladesh still persist in living on the flood plains). The danger is not only from the molten rock, which usually moves relatively slowly, but also from the release of harmful gases and the showers of red hot ash that destroy anything they touch (NB, the destruction of Pompeii and Herculaneum in AD 79, where people just had no time to avoid the ash storm and were effectively incinerated where they stood. Mount Vesuvius gave very little warning, and the eruptions probably claimed some ten thousand lives. People were choked by poisonous fumes before the ash, which eventually reached a depth of ten meters, finally destroyed them.)

The deadly effect of a combination of hot gas and ash particles known as a pyroclastic flow travels very rapidly and catches people unaware. Nowhere was this more evident than in the explosion of

Mount Pelee in Martinique early in the twentieth century. Originally regarded as something of a lush tropical paradise in what was the French West Indies, everything changed when its principal city was virtually incinerated one May morning in 1902. Nothing had been heard from the volcano since 1851, and in the intervening years inhabitants did not take the occasional rumblings too seriously. But when the explosion finally happened, it virtually destroyed the city and claimed an estimated thirty thousand lives.

Mudslides due to volcanic activity, though rare, can also be devastating. In 1985, at Nevado del Ruiz in Columbia, heat from a volcano generated an avalanche of mud and glacial water that is reckoned to have killed some twenty-three thousand people, some in towns as far as fifty kilometers from the volcano. It is true that the possibility of mudslides is enhanced by the understandable but irresponsible practice of deforestation. But it is rather hard in circumstances like these to blame people for their own deaths.

For the violent effects of tsunamis, one has to look no further than the explosion of Krakatau in Indonesia in 1883. Very fortunately no one lived on this small volcanic island between Java and Sumatra when its volcanic cones exploded; two-thirds of the original island disappeared, leaving an undersea crater nearly three hundred meters deep. The disaster began with a series of minor explosions in May that increased in periodicity and intensity until 27 August, when there were four climactic explosions that were actually heard in Australia, 3,224 kilometers from the eruption. The detonation was so violent that plumes of ash reached the stratosphere. The pyroclastic flow of hot gas and ash particles, perhaps travelling on mats of floating pumice, swept across 30 meters of sea and incinerated 3,000 people living near the coast of Sumatra.

But the most devastating effects were produced by the tsunamis. These too began in a small way, precipitated by the early minor explosions. But with the main eruption, gigantic waves thirty meters high inundated the region's coastal areas (the effects were so powerful that one ship was swept into a forest inland, where it remained until 1979 when it was cut up for scrap metal). The principal tsunami took just eleven hours to reach distant Honolulu, and tide levels were actually affected around much of the world. It is estimated that, in all, thirty thousand people lost their lives in what in geological terms was a mere burp of nature. But it left a gruesome legacy of pumice and human remains that reached as far as East Africa. In 1928 a new volcanic cone emerged from the sea on the original site, which was given the name Anak Krakatau (child of Krakatau), and as recently as 1995 it was seen spewing ash into the sea. Even yet Krakatau is not extinct.

Does any more really need to be said about what is sometimes called "natural evil"? The term, as we shall see, is often seriously disputed because it connotes something which implies intention and deliberation, almost as though nature were consciously conspiring against its own creatures. Most people—if they think about it at all—probably just accept nature as a fact of life, neither good nor bad. A morally neutral sine qua non of our existence. But for religious believers, most particularly monotheists, it cannot be seen in such simple terms. Their doubts are not so much about the cosmos in general—a subject that is almost entirely beyond our comprehension—but about our "island home." In other words, the Special Creation hypothesis. Our task, then, is to look at some of the responses to the problem that have been given by the good and the great to see if they bring us any nearer to an answer. Then we must consider the critical issue of moral evil.

But first a look at one version of the free-will argument, in this case what is rather elaborately called the "free process defense" but which really does not have anything new to say (see Hebblethwaite 1976). The argument is simply that God allows the physical world to "be itself," in other words, to let evolution take its course. This is said to be not a world in opposition but in "independence."

This is surely an argument from theological desperation. We must reject the notion of some apologists (e.g., Worsley 1996) that although "natural evil is rarely dependent upon the immediate structural requirements of the human brain (the connection is an indirect one), [t]he human brain is the product of an evolutionary process which is sufficient for natural evil" (96). The further argument that natural disasters and disease are contingencies of the evolved world as we know it is, admittedly, incontestable. (Worsley, in fact, argues that both earthquakes [vulcanism] and cancer—or their possibility—are necessary to the evolved world. Is this a contingency beyond divine ingenuity?) But the argument from theism that the Creator is necessarily bound by the processes and biochemistry of the evolutionary process that has been created seems to be a contradiction in terms. Furthermore, the view that speciation (variety) and freedom are intended or desirable products of evolution is also open to doubt. This kind of post-facto reasoning simply takes life as it is as life as it must be and works backward in a doggedly determinist fashion in order to find the answers. Contrary to some theistic scientists, creation may not be a seamless garment. It may be conceded that evolution implies costs, but what kind of costs, and how many costs? Life, precious as it is, can be prohibitively expensive.

There is a tendency on the part of the process theorists to try to remedy the situation by switching the focus from a creator deity to an *already* existing deity who is therefore not ultimately responsible for the natural order but who could possibly do something to modify/alleviate the unwelcome conditions that exist. This is an unconvincing escape mechanism which merely puts the problem back one notch. The problem remains: if there is a powerful deity who can help, why isn't that help forthcoming?

It is quite frustrating for the inquirer to find modern theorists looking for answers by reformulating the question or by redefining the terms. It is also unrewarding to discover that they often resort to postmodernist ingenuities in terms of "narrative" discourses that can only be understood in terms of their cultural context, e.g., "forms of life and sociohistorical configurations" (Surin 1986, 27). Important as this is—and I say this as a sociologist—it can result in just an elaborated form of old-fashioned relativism. Do different cultures in different ages *really* differ that much on what constitutes evil?

Process theory (à la John Polkinghorne) is all very well-meaning from a theistic point of view, but it takes as its basic assumption the idea, or hope, that our world has been created for some ultimately good purpose. Somehow everything, including disease, death, and natural disaster must all somehow conduce to a good end. It is the final outcome that matters, regardless of the indescribable pain of achievement. This is all justified in terms of "continuing creation"—an activity that is "hidden . . . within the unpredictable flexibility of the cosmic process" (Polkinghorne 1989, 44). One has to question the idea that it is specifically providential to allow the physical world "to be itself . . . [as] Love's gift of freedom" (66). About the evolution of the cosmos, we have little choice. As to the ultimate intention, it can only be an effrontery to presume that it is for *our* benefit.

John Barrow has pointed out that we have to draw a clear distinction between the laws of nature and the outcome of those laws. The fact that the outcomes of such laws "need not possess the symme-

tries of the underlying laws makes science difficult and teaches us
why the complicated collective structures we find in nature can be
the outcomes of simple laws of change and invariance" (Barrow
1999, 128). Perhaps for "simple laws" we should here read "elegant
laws." After all, it is only in the life sciences that we find the simple
laws of selection and adaptation that appear to govern the evolutionary process. No such principle appears to govern the fundamental
physical sciences. But whether we can regard the mathematical values that underlie the nature of the cosmos as "simple" is yet to be
determined. Regardless of any serious reservations we may entertain
about nature, these mathematical values seem to be evidence of a
deep logic within the universe.

# 2

# Moral Evil One: Violence and Values

I HAVE FOUND IT INTERESTING, AND NOT A LITTLE DISTURBING, THAT IN A recent *Dictionary of Modern Thought* there is no reference to evil (even under "Soul," I found only allusions to certain forms of American blues music!). Ethics, which we are about to discuss, *is* mentioned, but not morality. Presumably this is because the term has acquired normative and therefore prescriptive connotations that in the modern secular world are socially taboo. Many religious people are still prone to ascribe evil to some kind of external agency (the Devil, Satan, the Adversary, etc.), while secular theorists are prepared, à la Freud, to attribute evil to the as-yet uncivilized facets of our animal natures, something that time and social development (and therapy?) will hopefully cure. Some theorists, on the other hand, are inclined to dismiss the idea as some kind of psychological abberation, while for other social theorists, evil equals that which receives social disapprobation, and social disapprobation tends to change with the times, the culture, and the situational context.

So is that all there is to it? Are there no objective standards whereby we can judge human action? In other words, are there no such things as objective moral values? Are all values relative?

Values, including moral values, may be defined as objects of need, attitude, or desire which may be expressed as behavioral imperatives. Few people would dispute that values are important. They lie at the very heart of social experience. They are implicit in just about everything we do, yet it is extremely difficult to adduce scientifically valid criteria for assessing even the most common values. Ideologies, whether religious or otherwise, are really constellations of values and beliefs that are arguably independent—contra Marx—of the material conditions of life. Indeed, they can be instrumental in the formation of social arrangements for which they may provide the appropriate rationale.

The appropriation and utilization of values is one thing, but how they derive presents us with one of the thorniest problems of all. It has already been argued in some detail that there are only three logical "solutions" to this problem (Carlton 1995, 16ff.). Values must either be personal (innate), extrapersonal (social), suprapersonal (metaphysical), or some variant or combination of these. The personal "solution" is fraught with difficulties because it is, in turn, conditioned by the further problems of conflicting subjectivities (I think A, but he thinks B. On the other hand there is always C, etc, etc.). The extrapersonal "solution" is much beloved of social scientists. Though popular, it also raises all sorts of awkward questions, not least that of whether there is some confusion between the value *per se* and its social expression. What is being suggested here is that a value may not be culturally relative but a fundamental "object of desire" such as social status (esteem), which finds different forms of expression in different societies. Here we are on something of an intellectual roundabout because the argument that values can only derive from social experience simply presents us with an irritating circularity.

The suprapersonal solution has, of course, strong other-worldly implications. It doesn't find much favor in a post-religious society simply because its claims are unproved and presumably unprovable. It suffers too from the tendency of some advocates of trying to substantiate nonempirical statements such as "religion is good" by empirical generalizations such as "religion is universal." This does not follow logically, although, as with many other consensus arguments, it can be persuasive. The idea of "revealed" values suggests ultimate verities which lie outside the academic orbit and most probably belong to the realm of philosophical and theological speculation. Yet it would certainly be presumptuous to insist that all values are merely human contrivances, that is, devices concocted for the sake of social harmony. This tends to ignore such generally acknowledged, if not always observed, values such as truth-telling, justice, loyalty, reciprocity, and the like, which are critical to our existence. In very broad terms, we adhere to such values because the world works better that way.

If, therefore, such values make sense, and if the abrogation or denial of such values leads to pain and distress, can we justly refer to this as moral evil? And are we here thinking of negative or positive evil—sins of omission or sins of commission? It is interesting that the word sin—an old-fashioned but still meaningful term—is sometimes thought of as "missing the mark" (in Greek, "harmartia"), a kind of inadvertent failure. The image, originally taken from military training, is that of an arrow falling short of the target simply because the archer made a misjudgement and didn't aim high enough. As far as moral behavior is concerned, this is surely true of us all. Yet the notion of omission has exculpatory implications and suggests that we really can't help being the way we are.

It is here that we encounter the problem of determinism, about which theorists have debated interminably. Determinism may be defined as the belief that everything that happens has a cause or causes, either *necessary* (contributory) causes or *sufficient* (total) causes and could not have happened differently unless something in the cause or causes had also been different. The argument is that events must be what they are or will become by virtue of the forces that necessitate them. Indeed, it is difficult to see how science could proceed without making such assumptions. (Note, however, that we are still not sure to what degree this obtains in the quantum world, although some physicists speculate that there is an underlying certainty to the apparent indeterminacy of subatomic particles.)

But what of the behavioral world? If the more extreme advocates of determinism are right, does this mean that we are no longer responsible for our actions? Or can it be persuasively argued that regardless of all the identifiable antecedent factors to any acts there will always be the individual's conscious decisions to do what he or she did? So when recently a group of youths—including a girl—repeatedly raped a chance acquaintance on a towpath and then threw her body into the river (a terrible experience from which she surprisingly survived), were they simply "compelled" by antecedent factors? Are we talking about a theoretically predictable conjunction of events? Was choice not an option? Can it be plausibly maintained that their upbringing, education, subcultural norms, and so forth, are sufficient to explain their behavior? The difficulty with this kind of argument is that it leads to an infinite regression. Before we know where we are, we are back at the dawn of history.

Theoretically, there is no final answer to the problem of determinism because, even if we insist upon the primacy of the will, we have to ask why do we will what we will when we will it? Can we construct a meaningful train of events, a plausible hypothesis? This is a task that is often attempted, with varying degrees of success, as exculpatory exercises in the criminal courts. But ultimately it is difficult to avoid the issue of personal responsibility. We may accept theoretically that we are subject to deterministic forces, but we all act *as though* we have free will (e.g., I find it hard to believe that I couldn't have written that last sentence differently, if I'd wanted to, and that I wrote it precisely the way I did because, given all the antecedent factors of my life and experience, I really had no choice).

Surely when we think of evil we are contemplating something more than sins of omission? We rightly exercise a certain skepticism when we are told that those who commit heinous crimes do so because they are victims of unfortunate circumstances or driven by inexplicable inner compulsions. There are undoubtedly those who would be diagnosed as psychotic and psychopathic (however we define those terms), who either do not seem to be able to make "normal" moral distinctions or who find such distinctions meaningless. But these comprise a tiny minority.

Much more disturbing are those who are aware of the received codes but who for reasons of self-interest either choose to ignore them or reinterpret them in order to further their own purposes. It is in this connection that we are going to consider the exploits— sometimes applauded in exemplary terms—of some of history's well-known leaders, and of those who carried out their instructions, and ask if these are examples of organized moral evil.

What are we to make, for example, of the estimated 150,000 people who were involved, one way or another, in the Holocaust program? Not all were active killers. Heinrich Himmler, the Reichsfuhrer SS, the chief architect of the program, never actually killed anyone—he just gave the orders. This vast system of mechanized murder required an extensive administrative machinery of sundry officials and clerical assistants. Furthermore, the industrial hardware of death had to be tendered for, designed, manufactured, and delivered (many of Germany's most prosperous firms, such as Siemans and I. G. Farben, were infamously involved in the process). And what of those who comprised the *Einsatzgruppen*—the killing squads—who operated on a massive scale in Poland and Russia prior to the rationalized murder machinery of the death camps? Several thousand SS/SD (security police) and their auxiliaries operated in this way behind the lines in 1941–42, killing without apparent compunction on command. Were they all brutal, ignorant psychopaths with uncontrollable urges? Hardly. In fact, some of their leaders (for example, Otto Ohlendorf and Franz Six) were highly qualified intellectuals, lawyers, and administrators (see Hohne 1969).

Surely no one can view such a system as anything but inherently evil? German policy in the East (Poland and Russia) was not the result of wartime exigencies. Total repression was the plan from the beginning. It was a system of maximum exploitation of material and human resources. First there was the extermination of intellectual, political, and religious leaders in Poland. The population was to be reduced by servile labor and the liberal application of sterilization techniques that were being perfected by experimentation in the concentration camps. It was in Poland too that the death camps were set up, in this case utilizing the technique of "mercy killing," which had already been tested on the mentally sick in Germany itself. The Germans administered much of Poland from the area designated the "General Government," which was directly involved in the program of exploitation and mass slaughter. Besides the Holocaust victims, thousands died of hunger and disease and, not least, as victims of reprisals.

If anything, the policies pursued in Russia were even more horrendous. Hitler had made it clear to his generals that the war against the Soviet Union from June 1941 onwards was to be prosecuted without mercy against the untermenschen (Slavs and Jews). Russian prisoners of war were starved and beaten to death; certainly somewhere in excess of two million did not survive internment. Perhaps as many as 1,250,000 Jews and other "undesirables" were massacred between 1940 and 1942 by various murder squads, including the four *Einsatzgruppen* ("action groups" which were, in effect, extermination groups), before the gas chambers were established. The German intention was to create a slave state that would exist solely to provide Germany with foodstuffs and raw materials (Weinberg 1994).

Such plans may well have originated with Hitler and the SS/SD and been inspired by Nazi ideologues such as Alfred Rosenberg, but the plans were implemented by military leaders who were only too willing to carry out these instructions. The SS/SD plus various police units and sundry Ukrainian and Baltic volunteers have rightly shouldered much of the blame, but they should not be seen as the "alibi of a nation" (Reitlinger 1956). German military units and particularly the Waffen (military) SS were very much involved in many of the massacres. Again, we are not speaking of psychotics and psychopaths, but men (and in some cases women) who, with a few notable exceptions, were obeying orders that they presumably felt were right.

Nazi policy necessitated intimidation of smaller European states, and aggressive war against those that required the application of what the generals judged to be invincible military force. And it has to be admitted that aggression often pays. One has only to recall the approval that greeted the declaration of war by Germany in 1914, and even more so the early victories of the Axis powers in 1939–42. These events received overwhelming endorsement from their own peoples, and neutral states such as Sweden and Switzerland were morally compromised by their opportunistic cooperation in the Nazi litany of conquests.

In war everybody suffers, combatants and noncombatants alike, if not from wounds then from consequent famine and disease. Indeed, in modern war all may be considered to be equally guilty. Note particularly the Allied air offensive policy from 1942 onward; area bombing meant the deliberate killing of civilians (who might well be industrial workers) as well as the attempted destruction of military targets (Hastings 2000). So thousands were killed in places such as Dresden and Wurtzberg, which had no obvious strategic value. (Note here the predominant use of incendiaries to create firestorms among civilian housing, as opposed to high explosive that was normally used against military targets). The justifying assumption appears to have been that all Germans had supported Hitler, so all were "under condemnation." It was a question of ensuring that those who had so cruelly sown the wind should therefore "reap the whirlwind." The judges in the postwar Nuremberg Trials agreed that the crime of the Nazis and their allies was not only the way in which the war had been conducted but the fact that it had been initiated at all (see Carlton 2001, 125–38).

Although the rationalized system of extermination organized by the Nazis was unique and, indeed, one of the greatest crimes in history, *in principle* it was nothing new. Aggressive war and mass slaughter have sadly been a recurring feature of the human race. Again, they can be associated with military conquerors often numbered among the great commanders of the past, such as Alexander the Great, Pompey, Julius Caesar, Richard Coeur de Leon, Napoleon, and leaders such as Stalin, Pol Pot, and Mao Tse-tung. Here again we have also to lay blame on their subordinates, the all too willing soldiery (or should we say executioners?) who carried out the tasks. Often these "incidents" and mass slaughter will not be seen as examples of moral evil, but merely as the exigencies of war. This itself is an extension of the power game in which death is regarded as an unfortunate corollary.

Before we look for explanations, perhaps we should glance at some of the exploits of these heroes of history and ask ourselves whether we are confronting moral evil or whether we are merely witnessing the policies and practices of expediency.

Alexander is still regarded as one of the greatest military commanders of all time, a hero to schoolboys, and applauded as conqueror of Persia, then a vast and oppressive world power. Alexander began his auspicious career with murder. He was jealous of his father, Philip, king of Macedon (himself no mean performer in the expansionist stakes), and may well have been complicit with his mother, Olympias, in Philip's assassination (338 BC). Whatever the case, Alexander quickly had the assassins executed, possibly to prevent anyone knowing exactly who had issued the "contract." Once he assumed power, nothing was going to be left to chance. He and his mother ensured that any rival claimants (including Philip's latest wife and her infant son) were conveniently dispatched.

Barely out of his teens, Alexander now determined to reassert Macedonian supremacy throughout mainland Greece. At first, he successfully subdued certain tribal elements, and then, in league with a number of cooperative minor city-states [poleis], he tackled Athens, which he treated with uncharacteristic leniency, before turning his attention to Thebes. Some 150 years before, Thebes had given aid to the invading Persians, and this, in Alexander's view, entitled this "medizing" state to just, if belated, punishment. And it is here that we see the signs of the burgeoning despot. With the opportunistic support of some neighboring states of Thebes (Orchomenos, Phocis, Plataea, and Thespiae), who had no love for Theban hegemony, the Macedonians attacked the city. Thebes, one of the largest and most powerful of the Greek poleis, was virtually destroyed. Some six thousand people were butchered, and another thirty thousand were sold into slavery. Northern Greece was so intimidated that, in the state of Arcadia, those who advocated giving aid to Thebes were actually condemned to death. But then internecine strife was a popular Greek pastime.

The massacre had its desired effect; Alexander was now both admired and feared throughout the country. With a relatively small (possibly forty thousand) but highly trained army that was one of Philip's legacies, Alexander embarked upon what was to be his life's work, the conquest of Persia. But why? For many years Persia had exerted undue influence in Greek affairs, and her gold was often found subverting the interests of various poleis. Neither the Greeks nor the Persians had quite forgotten their historic wars (490–79 BC), so it is perhaps understandable that the Macedonians, who were arguably only Greeks by association, should have thought that a campaign was called for. But underlying this grand design, which was originally Philip's, lay a lust for the fabled wealth of the "Great King" (of Persia). It was a venture that was to wreak havoc throughout the Middle East.

With his considerable victories (and more were to come) Alexander began to see himself as something more than an ordinary human being and therefore not subject to the normal constraints of human behavior. As a divine or semi-divine being, he was not to be frustrated in his self-appointed mission. So when he decided on a diversion to the Phoenician-dominated coast of Palestine, it was presumably to neutralize the city-states that were within the Persian sphere of influence. Here his specific intention was to subdue the cities of Tyre and Gaza. The siege of Tyre, an island city just off the coast, took seven months—an inexcusable delay in the conqueror's timetable—and therefore merited appropriate punishment. The troops were allowed to pillage and murder at will. Some eight thousand defenders died, and a further two thousand were gratuitously crucified (four hundred or so Macedonians were killed, some, admittedly, while still prisoners of the Tyrians). But retribution did not stop there. As at Thebes, some thirty thousand were sold into slavery. The only people that were spared were the king and some city dignitaries who had taken refuge in the temple of Herakles, the Greek deity to whom Alexander afterward offered sacrifice (Arrian 1971). A similar fate befell Gaza. The siege engines were brought down from Tyre, and the battle-frenzied Macedonians made short work of the city. Every one of the defenders was killed, and the women and children were sold as slaves. The conqueror had now become the "sacker of cities."

Militarily speaking, Alexander was something of a genius: calculating and innovative, while his personal bravery was an example to his men. But he also had his dark side. His almost unbroken success increased his sense of divine infallibility. Like so many similar despots and would-be dynasts, he became pathologically suspicious. He saw plots here, there, and everywhere—a tendency not helped by his increasing dependence on alcohol (O'Brien 1992). Toward the latter part of his mercifully short career, he had six hundred of his own men executed (including high-ranking officers) because he claimed to have uncovered a far-reaching conspiracy. Perhaps it was as well that he died when he did (either of a fever or possibly by poison) because it was rumored that after having come to grief in India he was planning further conquests in the West.

Aggressive war—that is, completely unprovoked war—is really a form of mass murder. And yet many of those who have been responsible for this kind of carnage are often listed among the great personalities of the past. They are frequently applauded for their statesmanship and military acumen, but their cruel and irresponsible acts are either not that well known or are actually ignored. Moral evil on a massive scale simply comes with the job.

A classic example is that of Julius Caesar and his contemporary military dictators. At the time Caesar was born (possibly 100 BC), Rome was going through a period of fraticidal civil strife. This is the era known as the Late Republic, when the dynast, Marius, who had been successful in countering coalitions of northern barbarians as well as in subduing various North African (Numidian) tribes, was seeking yet again to be elected consul. But even after his welcome reorganization of the Roman army, his career suffered a temporary eclipse. When he finally returned to power (87 BC), he adopted a much more radical stance, and in order to secure his position had a number of his political rivals executed, especially among the Optimates (representing the ruling classes). He died only a year later, having been elected consul for an unprecedented seventh time. The mantle of military despot was then assumed by another "strong man," Cornelius Sulla, who—if anything—was more ruthless than his predecessor. He too was an extremely able general who had a notable success against one of Rome's most notorious enemies, Mithridates of Pontus, who in 88 BC had ordered a form of fatwa against all Romans and Italians living in Asia Minor. This was a political rather than a religious edict that was taken up with alacrity by his people and resulted in the deaths of some eighty thousand people. Sulla crushed the rebellion (85 BC) and as punishment imposed a virtually unbearable indemnity of twenty thousand talents, for which, ironically, the guilty states had to turn to Roman bankers for loans.

Sulla returned in triumph to a Rome that was in political turmoil in 83 BC. He took his legions to the city (something forbidden in Roman law) and set about "rationalizing" the situation by dealing unmercifully with his opponents. Ignoring normal constitutional precedent, he had some sixteen hundred put to death, including seventy members of the ruling Senate (Keaveney 1982), and soon afterward uncharacteristically retired from public life (79 BC). His career and that of Marius, together with those of the up-and-coming dynasts, Pompeius (Pompey) and his arch-rival Caesar, perfectly exemplified the fact that it just didn't pay to be on the wrong side in Roman politics.

Rome was ridden with factional rivalries, most conspicuously between the Optimates and the Populares (the representatives of the people). It was a kind of class conflict that ambitious men exploited to their advantage. Pompeius came to prominence by crushing the Populares, whom he had once supported. Many were executed, but when the bloodshed got out of hand, the Senate (virtually an Optimate foundation) began to have second thoughts about the military leader they had chosen as their champion. But few people in Rome had clean hands. Some years before, the Republic had enjoyed a period of unprecedented expansion and prosperity. Wealth and slaves followed upon its extensive conquests. Sardinia was occupied, entailing the death and enslavement of eighty thousand people (177 BC). Ten years later it was the turn of Epirus in northwestern Greece, with some 150,000 victims. In 146 BC, the year that Carthage was finally defeated in the interminable Punic Wars, a wholesale campaign was conducted in central Greece in which Corinth was destroyed. The influx of slaves was enormous. They were wanted for public works, for the spectacle of deaths euphemistically called the Games, and for the lucrative slave trade generally.

By the following century, slaves had become such a problem, especially in the large slave estates [latifundia] in Italy and Sicily, that revolts became endemic. And it was in relation to the most famous of these, in 73–71 BC, that Pompeius cemented his unenviable reputation. The ex-gladiator Spartacus, a Thracian who had once served in the Roman army, had raised a rebellion that devastated parts of Italy. The rebels had even defeated several legions until they faced the combined forces of Pompeius and Crassus, a wealthy aristocrat who had overall responsibility for the campaign. The rebels were totally defeated, and after the initial slaughter, as a salutary example to other recalcitrant slaves, the victors lined the road from Capua to Rome with six thousand crucified survivors. And the city of Rome rewarded them with a celebratory triumph in honor of their achievement.

Henceforth, Pompeius, who patently saw himself as another Alexander, went from triumph to triumph. His conquests, especially in the Near and Middle East, resulted in the capture of nearly three hundred kings and princes and in 61 BC brought him the accolade

"Pompey the Great, Conqueror of the World." But, as so often happens, the darling of the mob can become an object of dislike and distrust, especially by the Senate, whose members were increasingly suspicious of his true motives. Did he intend to set himself up as dictator? Within twelve months, Pompeius had become the victim of his own success and was largely impotent once his legions had been disbanded.

The no-longer-youthful but extremely ambitious Julius Caesar now found that his time had come. He took advantage of incipient jealousies and allied himself to the influential Crassus, a one-time Sulla protégé. Together they undermined the popularity of Pompeius, who had once been the senior partner in their small political coalition or triumvirate which had been formally confirmed by judicious intermarriage. Having agreed upon a convenient division of labor in relation to official appointments (dutifully endorsed by a hesitant Senate), they went their separate ways. Caesar had a governorship in Spain from which he was able to pay off his enormous debts incurred in bribing his way to office. The Senate then tried to fob him off with a "harmless" proconsular appointment. But in 59 BC he obtained, though as yet untried, a military command in Gaul—an astute move. Though now in middle age, in this way he made his reputation as an able and ruthless commander against the always threatening migratory tribes of the North.

Caesar's *Commentaries,* written some time after his campaigns against the Gauls and various Belgic and Germanic tribes, are the only substantial record of events. They were written primarily as an attempt to justify his actions to the Senate, whose members had good reason to suspect his political ambitions. The Commentaries are therefore hardly self-critical, but they do give a clear and concise account of events, as Caesar wished to portray them. They depict Caesar as a skilled and enterprising leader who enjoyed the full confidence of his men. He was fighting against brave but militarily unsophisticated warriors who attacked en masse in vast numbers, intent on securing their trophy heads, but they were no match for the better-equipped, disciplined men of Caesar's legions.

At times the carnage was fearful. Caesar tells how on one occasion he, like Alexander, gave his men their heads, and that this resulted in the massacre of 430,000 refugees. It is obvious that this was not done on impulse; it was all part of a calculated policy of intimidation in order to obviate further acts of insurrection. On another occasion, he reports that he had almost "blotted the name of the Nervii

[a tribe on the Franco-Belgium border] from the face of the earth"
(Caesar, 1951, 88). Of the sixty thousand or so men capable of bear-
ing arms, we are told that only five hundred survived. And when Caesar's legions defeated the Aduatuci, also in Belgium, the 350,000
tribespeople who survived the onslaught were all sold into slavery.
The Gauls and the Germanic warriors could be quite merciless to
their own prisoners, but it is disputable whether they merited this
kind of treatment.

It is, of course, possible that these figures are exaggerated. But
even that is significant. Caesar was obviously intent to impress his
readers and to justify his future claim to the dictatorship. By this
time his exploits outshone those of the now-fading Pompeius. Furthermore, the third member of the fragile triumvirate, Crassus, had
lost an army of thirty thousand against the Parthians in the Middle
East (53 BC) in an ill-advised attempt to emulate the military
achievements of his fellow triumvirs. Caesar then proved victorious
in the inevitable trial of strength with Pompeius (49–46 BC), and
then went on to indulge in another, but very different, game of wits
with the nubile Cleopatra, before returning to Rome and being as-
sassinated by his senatorial colleagues in 44 BC.

One could continue in this vein almost indefinitely. The ancient
world—indeed, the pre-industrial world generally—is replete with
the depredations of military conquerors and their rapacious followers. Moral evil of this kind is not the exclusive preserve of the modern world. And not just in terms of extent. It is true that modern
conflicts have brought death and suffering to greater numbers.
Modern weaponry and advanced technology have made sure of that.
(Wasn't it Aldous Huxley who said that the fruits of progress help us
to retrogress more efficiently?). But the pre-industrial world wasn't
far behind in the destruction stakes. It is not always appreciated, for
instance, that in the Middle Ages the Mongol hordes of Genghis
(Chingis) Khan created an unprecedented trail of murder and pillage. It is estimated that in China alone they left eighteen million
dead. And this was followed by successors, not least, Tamerlane
(Timur-Leng) and his Tartars who left hills of skulls in their wake.
The depredations of the Ottoman Turks, especially under Suleiman
the Magnificent, ran them a close second. And this was not a question of pressing a button to eliminate one's victims; this was all done
by hand.

Perhaps we could take one more example from the pre-modern
world, this time a man who is still applauded for his consummate

skill as a military strategist and tactician, Napoleon Bonaparte. Yet if there is anyone who indulged in needless aggressive wars it was this parvenu little Corsican. During the period of the French Revolution popularly—yet chillingly—known as the Terror, as an enterprising young artillery officer he played a major role in the recapture of royalist-held Toulon, which in desperation had gone over to the British (1793). He again came to the rescue of the government (Directory) when it was threatened by extremists. Thus his promotion was rapid, and at the age of only twenty-six he became commander of the French army in Italy. (Though this may well have been helped by his marriage to an older, aristocratic widow. In the game of politics a little hypergamy can go a long way.) His task was to drive the Austrians out of Italy and generally to secure France's borders at a time of considerable danger to its independence.

His dash and enterprise marked him out as a man with a future. He succeeded in either defeating or compromising various coalitions of hostile states and forced them to come to terms. Prussia and Spain made peace in 1795, although Britain—the traditional enemy—remained untouched, largely due to the near invincibility of its navy. The Directory wanted to launch an invasion of the British Isles, a venture which at this time Bonaparte regarded as a nonstarter. Instead he opted for what many years later some generals on Hitler's staff called the Mediterranean Strategy, i.e., attacking Britain indirectly by invading Egypt, and keeping India as a further option.

The first phase of the plan was almost entirely successful. Bonaparte captured Malta enroute and then defeated the Egyptians at the Battle of the Pyramids (1798). But a month later his fleet was virtually destroyed by Nelson at the Battle of the Nile. This seriously affected his supply route and effectively shortened the French army's period of occupation. It was in Egypt, where Bonaparte affected to respect the Muslim people, and where he evinced a genuine interest in ancient Egyptian culture, that he can be seen displaying the kind of brutality that his admirers tend to overlook. At first, he fleeced the Egyptian upper classes, who were forced to sell their property and valuables. Then levies were made on the merchant communities, and when this was insufficient there was the imposition of new taxes.

All this was in no way unusual for armies of occupation. But when protests were followed by local revolts, Bonaparte really began to turn the screw. Ringleaders were beheaded and villages were burned. Intimidation was the name of the game. He wrote to one of his subordinates that he was "having three heads cut off here every day and carried round Cairo; it is the only way to break the resistance of these people." And when a general revolt broke out in October 1798, he crushed the revolt in two days by a policy of wholesale butchery. As he instructed his chief-of-staff, "cut the throats of all prisoners taken with arms in their hands" (Barnett, 59–60). Their bodies were then to be thrown headless into the Nile. (A similar policy was also adopted against "rebels" in Spain in 1808). Bonaparte knew just how to win the hearts and minds of his subjects.

He continued to spread the glories of French culture by further conquests in Syria, the Lebanon, and Palestine (Israel). On his return to France (1799), he had to contend with coalitions of various European powers. This done, he replaced the Directory with a Consulate (1800), and effectively established himself as military dictator, a move that was reaffirmed by plebiscite. In 1804, in a complete turnabout for Revolutionary France, Bonaparte arranged for his own elevation to the monarchy, and once ensconced as emperor, his ambition was given free rein.

Elaborate preparations were made for an invasion of Great Britain, but these eventually came to nothing. Nelson's famous victory at Trafalgar in 1805 against the French and Spanish fleet neutralized Bonaparte's capacity to launch the cross-Channel assault he had so meticulously planned. But he drew some consolation from the fact that he was able to deal successfully with further continental complications. On the mainland his armies seemed invincible. He defeated an Austrian army at Ulm and then a combined Austrian and Russian force at Austerlitz, also in 1805, where, although outnumbered, his army inflicted twelve thousand casualties—an event which was later inflated by Bonaparte's hagiographers. Austria ceded territory as part of a peace settlement, which meant that France had extended her borders to include parts of Italy, Dalmatia, and Bavaria.

It is difficult to ascertain precisely who was principally responsible for the series of wars that followed, which cost countless lives. Probably most would agree that the primary blame rests with Bonaparte's inordinate craving for military glory and his desire to ensure France's great power status. But, at the same time, it must be conceded that revolutionary France, for a variety of reasons, generated a great deal of distrust and subsequent hostility from other European states. It was thus Bonaparte's intention to deal with them one at a time. He overwhelmed the Prussians at Jena (1806), who were also forced to surrender much of their territory. Furthermore, he instructed his paymasters to demand that Prussia paid for the war, which they did to the tune of 160 million francs. Indeed, by this time, Bonaparte had acquired so much territory that he was able to set up three of his brothers with modest—though not inconsequential—kingdoms of their own. He now controlled the Low Countries, most of Central Europe, Italy, Dalmatia, and part of the Baltic coast. Soon he was to command Portugal and part of Spain (although this was later successfully contested by a British expeditionary force under the Duke of Wellington).

There were resurgent attempts, especially by Austria, to wrest control from Bonaparte, but these only resulted in further humiliation. Yet he still had not been able finally to subdue Britain. Nor was he entirely successful against the Russians, who in their defense of Konigsberg destroyed a third of the attacking French forces (1807). But what he had managed to do was to order the European economy by means of the Continental System. This certainly had adverse effects on Britain, by restricting its ability to trade in Europe and, to some extent, overseas. This, in turn, hampered Britain's capacity to provide cash subsidies to European allies—its one way of undermining the power of the conqueror. But Russia proved recalcitrant. As an act of defiance, they refused to obey the rules. The Russians felt that they had a perfect right to do so. Why should they be told what to do by a foreign despot? It was this unwillingness to comply with the arbitrary ban on the importation of British goods which gave rise to yet another unnecessary and extremely costly campaign.

The master of Europe was determined not to be thwarted. Russian defiance might give other states dangerous ideas. Consequently, Bonaparte raised the largest army Europe had ever seen. He—like Hitler after him—was going to settle the Russian problem once and for all. But, also like Hitler, he failed to take sufficient account of the enormous distances involved, which presented serious logistical difficulties. And then there was the weather. The late autumn rains turned the roads, such as they were, into immobilizing muddy tracks. Meticulous preparations *for* war, as opposed to planning the battles themselves, had never been Bonaparte's strongest suit.

It should have been obvious from the outset that this was going to be no ordinary campaign. The Russians could afford to lure the French deeper and deeper into the seemingly limitless countryside, denying them the set-piece battle of which Bonaparte was the past master. Yet such an encounter could not be delayed indefinitely. So some seventy miles from Moscow the armies clashed at Borodino (1812). It was here that the Russians made a fruitless stand against the French, but they did inflict appalling losses on Bonaparte's Grand Armée which it could ill-afford.

When the French troops finally reached Moscow, they found it undefended. The deserted city was then set ablaze, but even this did not bring Russia's tsar to the negotiating table as Bonaparte had hoped. He waited until October, when the early snow had begun to fall and when the rivers of mud that had passed as roads were beginning to freeze over, making the return journey even more hazardous.

The subsequent retreat is now regarded as one of the epic stories of history—a tragic sequel to an entirely pointless campaign. The ill-prepared troops trudged wearily across the frozen wastes, permanently hungry and constantly harried by guerrillas and the remnants of Russian forces. The toll from starvation, frostbite, and enemy attack was catastrophic. Bonaparte had begun the trek to Moscow with something in excess of half a million men, of which less than a tenth returned home. The Grand Armée never really recovered; neither did Bonaparte's fortunes. He did—incredibly—raise another army, but it was a makeshift affair consisting largely of ill-equipped, ill-trained conscripts. And it was, once again, all so unnecessary. He still controlled much of Europe and could almost certainly have come to terms with his rival European states. But he had to go on; he had to try once again. The result was the disastrous battle of Leipzig and then Waterloo, and the effective end of Bonaparte's career. The tragedy is that, despite the incalculable suffering that he caused to his own people and to others, his memory is still not reviled. Volumes of reappraisal are still forthcoming, and the legend of the invincible conqueror inexplicably still lives on.

# 3

# Moral Evil Two: Persecution and Exploitation

WE CANNOT POSSIBLY CONSIDER EVERY CONCEIVABLE FORM OF MORAL evil, but few moral evils can be regarded as more important than war. Any study of the history of conflict bears this out. War undoubtedly brings out the best and the worst in people, though, arguably, there is such a thing as the "just war"—however this is interpreted. Some might contend that the worst forms of macro moral evil involve the persecution and extermination of vulnerable and defenseless people, which, admittedly, is often a corollary of war. Persecution and extermination, then, need to be further refined. In broad terms, we can say that mass killing tends to fall into one of three categories (or a combination or variant of these):

(1) *accidental*, as when Europeans unintentionally spread infectious diseases throughout conquered or otherwise-occupied territories. Such diseases as measles, which Europeans experienced in a relatively mild form, played havoc with indigenous peoples who had little or no immunity to such infections. Parts of South America and the Polynesian islands were devastated by these infections, for which the inhabitants had no natural defenses and the Europeans had no adequate remedies. Apologists have argued that various diseases, unknown to Europeans, were "exchanged" in return. This may be the case with certain venereal infections but is certainly true of the fatal diseases found especially in West Africa—the "White Man's graveyard."

(2) *incidental*, where—as we shall see in relation to parts of Spanish America—indigenes were often worked to death in less-than-human conditions. Here disease also played a large part and may have become, at certain times and in certain places, a cynical instrument of colonial policy. Into this general category we can also include the very worst features of slavery and the slave trade, again particularly in a West African context.

(3) *methodical*, where there is a deliberate plan to exterminate

whole groups of people, including genocide (technically the murder of an entire race, as with the Nazi Holocaust program, which
also included the incidental killing of slave laborers (Manchester
1969).

There seems never to have been a time when atrocities of this
kind did not take place. And it happened for a variety of reasons:
political, demographic, ideological, or just because one group was
bent on revenge against another. Some tribal societies such as the
Zulu and the Matebele in the early nineteenth century saw it as a
military norm. In certain circumstances, classical societies regarded
the killing of enemy males and the enslaving of their women and
children as a necessary expedient. Greeks would sometimes do this
to fellow Greeks in their inter-state [*polis*] wars, and the Romans
were certainly not averse to the practice as far as barbarian tribes
were concerned, as evidenced, for example, by the legions of the
Emperor Trajan and his treatment of the Dacians in what is now Romania.

In the Middle Ages, the depredations of the Vikings were a byword (including those of William of Normandy), and the wholesale
massacres by the Mongols and the Tartars were legendary (how
many other conquerors put entire cities to the sword, and left heaps
of severed heads in their wake?). But during the same period, there
were many lesser atrocities: those of the Crusaders and the Saracens
(see chapter 4, Moral Evil: Ideology and Expediency), for instance,
and those committed in the Hundred Years' War (note those atrocities attributed to Edward, the Black Prince, in France, not to mention
the extermination of French prisoners after the victory at Agincourt
by Henry V). One might pursue the medieval saga almost indefinitely, not omitting mention of the horrendous massacre of the
"heretic" Cathars and Albigenses, also in France at the behest of the
Papacy ostensibly for ideological reasons.

Nearer our own time, one could cite the atrocities associated both
directly and indirectly with the First World War. Of course, the war
itself was a form of mass murder—and quite unnecessary mass
murder, at that. It goes without saying that those responsible for ini-
tiating it—most notably the Austrians and the Germans—were quan-
titatively more culpable than the crassly incompetent generals on
both sides who ordered those acts of sheer folly that cost the lives of
thousands. To launch war is one thing; to conduct it as unimagina-
tively as in the First World War is tantamount to criminal indifference. It is probably true, as one critic has argued (Wolfe 1958), that

by 1916 few combatants really knew that they were fighting for. They just knew that they were there because they were there.

Yet not all the brutality can be attributed to those in command. The sentiment expressed in Erich Maria Remarque's well-known *All Quiet on the Western Front*, that all the politicians and generals of both sides should be put in a field so that *they* could fight it out together, is only part of the story. Moral evil also extended to the rank and file. Otherwise, how are we going to explain such incidents as those where wounded men who were inching themselves towards possible safety in a shell hole were deliberately picked off by enemy snipers? This certainly happened in one engagement in Belgium in 1917 where the Sixth Battalion of the Northumberland Fusiliers lost most of its men, including all but one of its forty officers. No mercy was shown even to the defenseless. (My own uncle was severely wounded by a dum-dum bullet while on patrol near the La Bassée Canal and crawled back to his lines under cover of darkness—later to be hospitalized for two years. No one could take any chances).

It is said that war brutalizes—or is the brutality incipiently present already? If anyone has any doubt, let us consider the now-well-authenticated German atrocities in Belgium in 1914. It has been long thought that such stories were fabrications or, at very least exaggerations, but the evidence clearly shows that they are substantially true.

Between the outbreak of the war in August 1914 and October 1914, the invading German troops shot and bayoneted 5,521 civilians in Belgium and just over 900 in occupied France (Horne and Kramer 2001). This does not include the scores of prisoners of war and the wounded, many of whom were also shot. Nor does it include the thousands of French and Belgian civilians who are known to have been deported. The German rationale for these patently inhuman acts was that those concerned were guilty of guerrilla activities and were therefore subject to the "rules of war." But it confounds the imagination how so many elderly people and children who were murdered could have been involved in this way. How, for example, can one fathom the reasoning that forced children to form a "human shield" (apparently a common tactic) which resulted in a hundred deaths? And why were 674 people massacred in Dinant (some ten percent of the population), including babies—an atrocity very reminiscent of the SS Das Reich's massacre of the people of Oradour in 1944? And this toll takes no account of the innumerable rapes and the torching of property that also attended the unwarranted German invasion.

What makes the whole sorry affair so puzzling for many, and has therefore occasioned furious denials, is that so many of the perpetrators were just young ordinary recruits from commonplace German homes. (Again, as at Oradour, many of the SS personnel were new recruits who were not even German.) The evidence indicates that these crimes were not confined to any particular regiment or unit but that such behavior seems to have been endemic to the German military and was not simply the work of lowlife, criminal elements. The view was that such acts were justifiable in "total war." What cannot be sustained is the thesis that such military attitudes are not so much attributable to discipline, fear, patriotism, or even ideology (which will be discussed in the next chapter) as to "masculinity." As though the proclivity to violence is exclusively a male preserve—a view unfortunately still promoted by some revisionist historians who wish to see life other than as it actually is (see Bourke 2001).

As we have seen, atrocities usually take place as part of a policy of repression by a dominant state. A particularly good example in recent years would be the oppression of the Kurdish population in Iraq by the regime of Saddam Hussein, which is known to have resorted to massacre on a large scale. But the phenomenon is hardly new. The practice of keeping a subject people in its place goes back a very long way—indeed, to the very earliest civilizations (note, for example, the subjection of the Nubians, the "non-people," by the ancient Egyptians in very remote times).

During the First World War, there was the now largely forgotten treatment of the Armenians by the more powerful Turks. Their "differences," which were religious rather than cultural, went back to the late nineteenth century, when part of Armenia was restored to Turkey by the Russian tsar. But the Armenians entertained nationalist aspirations and were promised reforms that didn't materialize. Soon their agitation became so vociferous that the Ottoman regime decided upon the radical expedient of extermination. In 1894 the Sultan (dubbed Abdul the Damned) decreed that all Muslims living among the Armenians were free to confiscate property and would be exonerated if they killed any Armenians who resisted. Poor Muslims seemed only too pleased to gain by the dispossession of others. The killings and torture were frightful; by 1896 it is estimated that one hundred thousand people died.

The Armenian people survived. Yet within a generation there was a repeat performance. The carnage of 1894–96 did not touch the

Turkish conscience enough to prevent further large-scale atrocities. The Ottoman regime, now irretrievably corrupt and in serious decline, took advantage of the distractions of the First World War to deal yet again with the Armenians. While most of the world was looking the other way, they launched a full-scale assault on the Armenian people. Leaders and intellectuals were arrested and deported. Then, as part of a deliberate government policy, mass executions were carried out. Women were sometimes spared, as were also some men if they professed conversion to Islam. There were many regional variations, but overall the policy was carried through with general genocidal intent. The killings, attended by starvation and disease, reduced the Armenian population from two million to about thirty thousand, yet few perpetrators were ever brought to justice for their monstrous crimes.

Persecutions and exploitation can fit into any one of these categories and can result in suffering and death that is accidental, incidental, and methodical. Colonialism—contrary to much popular thinking—has not been *all* bad. But it did often result in unspeakable suffering. Particularly indefensible was the subjugation and exploitation of the peoples of the Americas by European colonialists. It is clear that this took different forms in different places: infiltration and expropriation in North America, leading finally to social exclusion, and calculated repression in South America. In the north, it was mainly the British and the French who set the pattern for the future United States, whose policies and practices regarding the indigenes were just as ruthless-cum-paternalistic as those of its mentors. In the south, the actions of the Portuguese and especially the Spanish were particularly brutal and led to the decimation of whole swathes of the Indian population.

The Europeans can be rightly regarded as intruders, even invaders, although they liked to think of themselves as adventurers who were bringing the civilizing influences of European culture to pagan lands. The tendency today is to decry such claims as hollow and even duplicitous, and—complementarily—to portray the indigenous cultures as esteemable in their own right. Sometimes modern apologists like to depict the North American tribes as happy, carefree people until they were corrupted by unscrupulous foreigners. This is, needless to say, far from the truth. There were inter-tribal wars that, though not on a large scale, were often waged with considerable ferocity, and in which captives might be tortured for days before being finally put out of their misery (note particularly the

practices of the Iroquois federation of tribes on the eastern sea-
board). The Peruvian and Mesoamerican cultures were a different
matter. Their Spanish conquerors marvelled at their architectural
achievements but had nothing but disgust for Mesoamerican (most
notably Aztec) religious practices which involved an unparalleled
system of human sacrifice.

Racist beliefs were almost certainly held by many, if not most, of
the early colonizers. This was really quite understandable. After all,
the natives looked different, therefore, ipso facto, they *were* different. So it was a reasonable intuitive leap to suppose that these people were inherently incapable of achieving European standards of
culture. And where people believed that what they saw as savagery
was quite ineradicable—not helped, of course, by certain native
practices—repression was almost bound to follow. And follow it did,
with the effective destruction of the native economy and the deni-
gration of its supportive institutions. Tribal life, with its complex system of interrelationships, was undermined, and indigenous life
generally was edged to the margins of society.

With the coming of the Europeans, what had once been sporadic
warfare—in fact, largely attacks by raiding parties—among the
northern tribes tended to turn rather nasty. Warfare became more
extensive, often attended by atrocities on both sides. Indians butchered settlers who they felt had no right to their lands, and the whites
retaliated—often on a disproportionate scale with more sophisticated weaponry. And with the increasing influx of settlers things
could only get worse. Dispossessed and marginalized, victims of a
litany of broken promises, by the nineteenth century the imbalance
had become so great that the "red men" could no longer compete
and were forced to retreat to the reservations. White culture and
technology had won, and slowly—very slowly—the process of assimi-
lation had taken place.

The story of events in Mesoamerica and Peru is rather different.
The Spanish conquests in the early sixteenth century are an anoma-
lous combination of boldness and duplicity, of reckless courage cou-
pled with unexampled treachery. In the post-conquest phase, we
then find a considerable disparity between theory and practice, between religious ideology and the operationalization of that ideology—in short, a paternalistic concern in parallel with a regime of
ruthless repression.

The attitude of the Spanish toward the Aztecs of Mexico is, at
least, understandable. True, Hernando Cortés and his band of con-

quistadores were incredulous when they first saw the fabled Aztec
capital of Tenochtitlán (effectively, modern Mexico City). The city
and its organization were a source of admiration and wonder, quite
unlike anything they had ever seen or even anticipated (their early
encounters with the natives of Cuba had certainly not been anything
like this). But when they experienced at firsthand the horrendous
nature and scale of Aztec religious practices, they were disgusted
and repelled. Not that there was anything very different about such
practices in Mesoamerica. The Aztecs had inherited the practice of
human sacrifice from the earlier warrior Toltecs centered at nearby
Tula, and the practice was also found in other neighboring tribes,
including the Maya of the Yucatan, whose great days were now in
the past. Indeed, it was probably also known among the even earlier
Olmecs of the Santa Cruz area, although very little is known about
this seminal society. The only really exceptional thing about the
Aztecs is that they sacrificed on such a huge scale. In fact their wars
seem to have been waged not just for booty but also for potential
victims for the "stone" upon which their hearts would be torn out
and offered to the Sun—a singular honor—and their blood
smeared on the repulsive image of Huitzopochli, the War God. And
this was only one of the ritual niceties that were felt to justify the
depredations of the invaders, including the wholesale destruction of
the Aztec idols which they saw as instruments of the Devil.

Needless to say, Cortés's men were also intent on plunder. And
similarly—if not more so—was the even smaller army of another
soldier-adventurer, Francisco Pizarro, which arrived in Inca-
dominated Peru in 1532. With a force of barely 200 men plus an
assortment of disaffected rebels and tribesmen, Pizarro, by a mixture of bluff, guile, and ingenuity managed to conquer an empire.
It was an unbelievable achievement considering that the Incas commanded a territory stretching some 2,500 miles along the western
coastal region of South America. The treasures were vast (by 1990s
standards about £200 million). Torture and duplicity realized more
gold than the conquerors dreamed of (of which a fifth was to go to
the Spanish crown). And rumors still abound that yet more of the
fabulous wealth of the Incas remains to be found.

It took seven years to penetrate the Inca kingdom and another
five years finally to secure it. But the worst phase was to come. The
Spanish were determined to squeeze every ounce of silver and gold
they could from the Peruvian economy. The mines and the labor
were there, why not exploit them to the full? The Peruvians were

already used to an absolutist system, but—within reason—it was a benevolent despotism under which they could be sure of food and clothing. But this was hardly the case under the "enlightened" Spanish culture. Here the name of the game was extortion, and the prospects for reasonable living conditions were virtually nil.

It is not an overstatement to say that from now on it was a matter of misery, starvation, and death. The populations in some of the Peruvian valleys were reduced to about a tenth of their previous size. And it is estimated that by 1600 an overall population of approximately seven million had been reduced by starvation, disease (especially smallpox), and sheer oppressive labor (particularly in the mines) to less than two million. Understandably, such conditions proved intolerable to the natives, and a serious rebellion broke out in 1536 which lasted a year, and a second rebellion took place in 1539—conflicts that they couldn't possibly win and in which probably as many as twenty thousand people died. The Spanish, impatient with the surly, untamed attitudes of the Peruvians, launched a decisive campaign in 1572 in which the last would-be Inca ruler was executed, though not before he had made his appropriate confession and been baptized. The Spanish believed in making virtue of necessity.

It should, however, be borne in mind that in the long term the Spanish did bring certain benefits to their native subjects. Furthermore, there were those among the dominant culture who had a genuine concern for their charges, often (it has to be admitted) showing an inordinate zeal for the condition of their souls while ignoring the welfare of their bodies. On such matters, the Church, as ever, was at odds with itself.

It hardly needs to be stressed that one of the most inhuman forms of exploitation is slavery. But, as is so often the case, the term itself is subject to qualification. In earlier times, slavery was endemic to most societies in one form or another. Indeed, the classicist, Moses Finlay, has argued that freedom in anything like our sense of the term was virtually unknown, and that slavery was simply the lowest rung on an accepted hierarchical ladder. Certainly in classical Greek society there were at least six forms of bondage, ranging from the relatively well-placed household servant to the chattel slave who worked in chains in the Athenian silver mines or the Syracusan quarries, where life was nasty, short, and unquestionably brutish.

In similar forms, slavery can be seen in many societies before and since, particularly, as we have noted, in relation to the conquests of the Americas. However, to the modern mind, slavery tends to be associated with the African slave trade in which many European countries were involved. The earliest recorded incidents of slaving involved Arab traders and sundry entrepreneurs—ironic, really, considering the high regard in which certain protest movements, especially in the United States, have come to embrace Islam as the true faith of the black people. The trade was later taken up all too readily by the Europeans, most notably the Spanish, the Portuguese, the Dutch, the British, and the French (who were particularly reluctant to give up such a lucrative trade even after their defeat in the Napoleonic wars).

What is not always sufficiently appreciated is the degree to which West African tribes were complicit in the whole enterprise. It was they, at the instigation of their chiefs, who did most of the actual slaving among the tribes of the interior. This normally involved the raiding of villages, killing the old and the very young because they were of little value, and force marching the rest back to the coast, where they were then exchanged for European goods before being transported in inhumane conditions to the Americas. But slavery was hardly a European invention. It was certainly nothing new to the African tribespeople who had practiced slavery among their own people as long as anyone could remember (Gabel 1964). In fact, the coming of the Europeans heralded a more profitable phase in an age-old process. Blacks and whites were equally culpable. This makes the attempts of a consortium of modern black Americans to secure "compensation" for past slavery so ludicrous—let alone legally untenable. (But then the United States is the litigation state par excellence.) Given that slavery still exists in some Muslim states, perhaps some of the oil sheiks should also pay up for the misdemeanors of *their* forebears?

Moral evil is obviously not restricted to any particular culture, nor to any particular time. It is difficult, too, to go along with those learning theorists who maintain that much that we designate as evil (violence, aggression, etc.) is simply part of the growing pains of the human species. This view can hardly be sustained given our rather pathetic performance to date. There is really no convincing evidence to indicate that all we need is better education and a little encouragement and all would be well. History undoubtedly suggests otherwise.

Apologists among the deistic intelligentsia are unsurprisingly defensive about this. Their view is that if we are to have free rational beings then a predictably material environment with the possibility of evil (death and suffering) is an unavoidable necessity. But is it? Who has decided on a world of free, rational beings? Who is to say that this is the object of creation? Isn't this really just an extrapolation from accepted social mores? Furthermore, one must question the assumption that it is *we* who are the free, rational beings. A very good case can be made for the fact that we are not free in the psychosocial sense (with all his shortcomings, Freud may well have had a point here), and there is certainly no watertight argument against certain forms of historical determinism. We are all legatees of our antecedents. And as for rationality—surely experience tells us otherwise. Such optimistic notions about human nature derive from the surely mistaken view that derives from Plato that evil is merely the absence of good (I wonder how many Holocaust survivors would agree with that.) Or that "there are no such things as evil desires . . . only evil disproportion in our desires" (McCabe 2000, 623). Again, patently history and experience tell a very different story.

# 4
# Moral Evil Three: Ideology and Expediency

THE CATALOGUE OF INFAMY CONTINUES INTO THE MODERN ERA. CONtrary to the aspirations—indeed, the predictions—of some of our Victorian forebears, the world is not getting better. In many ways, despite the valiant efforts of well-intentioned humanitarians and the increasing perseverence of medical science, it is getting worse. Culture is open to question; demographic problems vitiate all efforts for social improvement; and amid all the high-sounding phrases of self-seeking politicians, the twentieth century has probably witnessed more bloodletting than any previous era, perhaps even more than all the wars of the preindustrial world put together.

Many years ago, the historian Arnold Toynbee produced his monumental study of history (1970), in which he presented a case for the rise and fall of civilizations. His views—no longer popular—are open to all kinds of criticisms (see Gardiner 1961), but they are certainly worth consideration. His underlying principle might be summarized as "nothing fails like success." As far as we can discern, there are no known laws that can be said to govern historical development, but it could be argued, as Toynbee does, that every good that has ever been achieved has been negated by some corresponding evil. In other words, for every gain there is a loss; every problem solved gives rise to even greater problems. (Certainly every question answered, especially in the world of science, generates yet further questions.) It is uncontentious to say that every effort to create a continuously growing, progressive civilization has failed—at least in certain critical respects. And if we ask why, it seems not unreasonable to argue that human beings through the ages have exhibited a seemingly infinite capacity for self-destruction.

Even democracy (and its institutions), often applauded as one of the most notable social achievements, has—in various forms—brought more problems than its advocates are prepared to admit. Its very inception in what is misleadingly called "democratic Athens" was fraught with internecine strife. It should always be borne in mind that ancient Athens, which boasted a radical democracy (i.e., having no executive, as such), was actually both more democratic (Assembly-governed) and less democratic (severely restricted representation) than anything we understand by the term. Indeed, the term democracy came to mean what "the people" wanted it to mean. In Athens, it meant repression. Weaker states were expected to follow suit and join the Athenian League which, in effect, was a minor empire with Athens as the main beneficiary.

Since these inauspicious early days, democracy, or what some call the People's System, has had a somewhat checkered career. What has actually been the experience of society when subjected to the anomalies and inconsistencies of the General Will? Jean-Jacques Rousseau, sometimes given the doubtful credit of being father of the French Revolution, once argued that the General Will is righteous and tends always to the public advantage. Needless to say, he modified his opinion in later life and would probably have repudiated it altogether had he lived to see the mindless excesses of the Terror in France (1793–94).

The "will of the people" is an extremely potent and persuasive idea. But what is it like in practice? In the aftermath of the Second World War, when other writers were rightly inveighing against totalitarianism, Bertrand de Jouvenal launched a particularly cogent attack against the view that People's Systems are inherently superior to other forms of political organization (1948). He pointed out that they have a number of serious disadvantages. They are notoriously susceptible to demagogic influences. Any persuasive rabble-rousers can use democratic platforms; note, for example, the Nation of Islam movement in the United States (and similar movements worldwide) that actually advocates the overthrow of the liberal democracy which allows its followers to express their subversive ideas. These are not a mile away from the traditional Wahabi-type fanaticism that caused the deaths of many thousands of people in New York and Washington in September 2001. Such outrages are the logical outcome of a perverted ideology.

There is also a definite correlation between People's Systems and the extension and magnitude of war. De Jouvenal argues, somewhat contentiously, that this has come about primarily because in earlier autocracies the essential controls were lacking, namely the power of conscription and the ability to impose taxes. This is not a very convincing argument because it can be shown that early autocracies were very tightly controlled, most notably where there was a pervasive ideology reinforced by a marked military presence. The evils of People's Systems—if such they can be called—are much more likely to be linked with demographic factors. This is by no means invariable, but there is no doubt that when population growth becomes unsustainable, trouble ensues, usually in the form of civil strife.

The People's System is, superficially, an attractive idea, replete as it is with heady notions of freedom and self-expression. But this may just mean the freedom to slaughter and to starve. What is much more insidious, especially in the modern world, is the tendency of rulers to use the themes of democracy and the General Will to mask their own ambitious "socialism." This has undoubtedly been used as a device to make totalitarianism more acceptable (note, National Socialism, the Union of Soviet *Socialist* Republics, the *People's* Republic of China, and so forth). There can, of course, be a "tyranny from below"—even despots must mobilize support. But the action of a People's System has often been something of a political fiction. It was Marx's alter ego, Frederick Engels, who once suggested that any state is an instrument of oppression, no less so in a democracy than in a monarchy. Indeed, it has been cynically claimed that democracies are worse in that they persuade the people to cut their own throats. The "people" are not necessarily right by virtue of just being the "people." Like the autocrats they often support, they can be wrong both morally and prudentially (see Carlton 1992, chaps. 1 and 2).

Moral evil is something for which we all have a special talent, but it is found most conspicuously in those leaders, military and otherwise, whose mortality rates literally run into many thousands, if not millions. No one fits this category better than Stalin, who controlled Russia's fortunes for the best part of thirty years. The Marxian inspired communism of those years was not quite the Rule of the People that many supposed. Marx's view was that "the people" have the potential capacity to constitute a revolutionary force within a capitalist society. Appropriately educated they have the ability to emancipate themselves. But once liberated, they are not fit to rule. They have to be properly led. We cannot, therefore, speak of equality for all—certainly not in the short term, and, as Maynard Keynes once acutely observed, in the long term we are all dead.

So leaders are necessary. Lenin in particular argued that an elite is essential to guide and educate the proletariat. Thus in Russian communism, as in other similarly organized states (Maoist China,

North Korea, Cambodia, etc.), the will of the people was simply a convenient disguise for a concentration of power in the hands of an autocrat.

After a virtually bloodless revolution in 1917, the Soviets withdrew from the war with the Central Powers (Germany, Austria, and their allies)—leaving the western Allies to face them alone—and set about trying to reconstitute a once-monarchical state. Eventually, they succeeded in replacing one despotism with another. At first, the Soviets struggled to survive. The revolution itself had been a rather haphazard, untidy affair carried out by a minority party led by a small group of individuals. Initially, few people—certainly in the West—wanted them to make a go of it. There were attempts to subvert the regime both from inside and outside Russia. But by a mixture of organizational skill, ideological zeal, and sheer ruthlessness, by 1923 it became clear that the principal leaders of the movement, Lenin, Leon Trotsky et al., were there to stay (Brooke-Shepherd 1998).

The tone of the regime was set early on by Lenin, who advocated the en masse elimination of the "enemies of the people." These comprised the usual classes of victims, landowners, distrusted intellectuals, and the like—anyone, in fact, who might be vaguely categorized as members of the bourgeoisie. The Cheka, the predecessor of the state security organizations, the NKVD and later the KGB, had the task of purging the country of "class enemies." And an attempt on Lenin's life provided an excuse for murder on a massive scale, especially in the Ukraine and in Petrograd (later, Leningrad) where five hundred people were shot.

Inevitably, doctrinaire socialism had to adapt somewhat in order to meet the exigencies of the situation. But no vested interests or rival organizations were allowed to develop that might challenge the prerogatives of the state—a blanket term for the ruling oligarchy. For at no time was there ever, as once envisaged, a dictatorship *of* the proletariat; there was ever only a dictatorship *over* the proletariat.

Lenin did not live to see the full flowering of the Soviet system, and Trotsky, his natural successor, was ousted in 1926 by Stalin, who had virtually come from nowhere to join the front ranks of the Party. Trotsky was driven into exile and spent the remainder of his life in fear of the man who had once occupied a modest secretariat position in the machinery of government. Stalin's plan to bring Russia into line with the highly industrialized West was formally initiated in 1928, and its first phase was completed in four years. But its land reform program (collectivization), although fine in theory, involved hardship for much of the peasant community, especially the more prosperous peasants (Kulaks) who suffered most from the state's repressive policies. Initially, collectivization had some success. The number of amalgamated farms nearly doubled in 1928–29. The very poor peasants had nothing to lose, and at first many formed committees to combat the power of the Kulaks. But when the Kulaks resisted they effectively ensured their own extermination when Stalin decreed that they must be eliminated "as a class."

On balance collectivization, which was ostensibly supposed to bring improved efficiency and greater social justice, actually brought nothing of the sort. In fact, it was an almost total disaster. Its calamitous effects were exacerbated by the failed harvests of 1931 and 1932, and the ensuing famine of 1933 resulted in the deaths of over three million people from disease and starvation. And if this were not enough, millions more who were classified as "class enemies" were either killed or sent to camps in the more inaccessible parts of the Soviet Union to be worked to death. The Revolution had been unbelievably expensive in human life. The total death toll by the mid-1930s has been roughly estimated at eight to ten million (Elliot 1973, chap. 3). Such figures must be somewhat conjectural, but who is going to quibble when the general picture is so compelling? Death and suffering on this scale seems to be almost mandatory with this kind of social engineering.

But there were also achievements. There was an enormous expansion of industry and consequently in production. Technical education had pride of place, but this still only benefited a minority. There was still widespread poverty; the Revolution had brought a burgeoning bureaucracy and a vast expansion in the armed forces, but, by and large, the ordinary people—the proletariat in whose name the revolution had been waged—were not markedly better off. One of the main problems, of course, was that the Soviet system was "socialism" in a hurry.

By the late 1930s, the focus of repression had switched from the now sufficiently cowed proletariat to the suspect or recalcitrant members of the military and the political elites. It is now recognized that the charges against the accused were almost entirely false. Like so many despots, Stalin could brook no opposition, so those closest to him were most in danger. There could be no rivals. So in 1934 the Leningrad Party boss, Sergai Kirov, had to go, almost certainly on Stalin's orders though the blame was deflected elsewhere. Then, in the fashion of organized crime, the hit men had to be hit. As Stalin himself put it, "the evil murder of Comrade Kirov [has revealed] many suspect elements within the Party" (quoted by Andrew and Gordievsky 1990, 101). This opened the door for a series of purges culminating in the "treason trials" of 1937–38 in which many of the persecutors became the persecuted.

The NKVD (euphemistically the People's Commissariat for Internal Affairs) was commanded by Genrikh Yagoda, who virtually had the power of life and death within the state. But he soon ended up on Stalin's proscription lists and was replaced by the diminutive but equally lethal Nicholai Yezhov. When the "traitors" were denounced, it can safely be assumed that the approval such condemnations received was tempered by the trial audiences' wish to remain alive. The charges were trumped-up for the occasion, and many— even in the West—were taken in by the abject "confessions" of the accused which were almost certainly extracted by intimidation and torture. (What would have happened to their families if they had refused? One assumes death or alternative accommodation in the gulag).

The numbers who suffered are incalculable. Consignment to a gulag was usually the same as a complete disappearance. For most it was a living death that could be finally ended simply by complaining about the conditions. The whole monstrous process of show trials and punishment went on unabated, with officials calling for more and more proscriptions (Yezhov personally went to the Ukraine to order thirty thousand more executions of class enemies—almost as though the local NKVD were not meeting the necessary quotas.) What was particularly bizarre were cases of relatives of victims calling for even greater government action against the "traitors." Soviet propaganda was such that many believed—or had believed—that the Party *must* be right.

Counterrevolutionary fervor claimed intellectuals and hundreds of upper military echelon personnel (little wonder the Red Army was in disarray when the Germans first invaded in 1941). In the spring of 1937 alone, over 300,000 political arrests were reported, and in the two years 1937 and 1938 the names of some forty-four thousand of those listed for execution were submitted to Stalin who, incidentally, did not attend the trials in person but is believed to have watched surreptitiously from behind a screen. The military elite was all but obliterated: three of five marshalls, thirteen of fifteen army commanders, eight of nine fleet admirals, 204 of 243 corps and divisional commanders, and—more surprisingly—ninety-nine of 108 political commissars, besides which there were thousands of dismissals (Conquest 1990, 450).

But most surprising was Stalin's assault on the NKVD itself. The main instrument of murder became the ultimate—and perhaps deserving—target of the dictator's morbid, paranoid suspicions. Yagoda had already met the penalty he had so readily meted out to others, and next came the fall of his replacement, Yezhov (shot with some 150 of his closest collaborators), who was succeeded by yet another accomplished executioner, Lavrenti Beria, who also followed suit after the death of Stalin in 1953. In all, the security police is thought to have lost about 3,000 of its members, but there were more than enough left to commit the infamous Katyn Forest massacre of Polish officers after the invasion of 1939. All too soon the ranks of the NKVD were opportunistically filled with those who were only too ready to kill to order both during "The Great Patriotic War" (i.e., 1941–45) when many military personnel were executed for "inefficiency," and afterwards when the persecution of yet more undesirables was carried out.

Statistics from both Western and Russian sources indicate that total arrests during the "Terror" were in excess of ten million (nobody knows just how many died in the Siberian camps), and probably about one million were executed. And these figures are quite apart from those given in Soviet sources concerning peasant repression (perhaps twenty million from 1929–33). Such was the legacy of the "father of the nation."

It is very difficult to know how much moral evil is the result of ideology, political expediency, or unashamed ambition. And what is particularly confusing is when one masquerades as another. In actual cases, it may well be a combination of all three with one element predominating—something that will vary from case to case. Whatever, in this section of the discussion we are going to concentrate on the overarching influence of ideology, both political and religious.

Because of its pervasive nature, and often insidious applications, we might continue to look at Communist ideology linked, as it usually is, to political ambition. This has led to some of the most infamous incidents in recent history. The quite unnecessary invasion of South Korea by the Communist North Koreans is a good example. Korea had been occupied for many years by the Japanese, whose regime was both rapacious and repressive—somewhat akin to their rule in China from the mid-1930s onward. Liberation came in 1945 with the defeat of Japan by the Allies who, admittedly, were at something of a loss to know just how to administer the territory. (The only people who knew anything about the language and had any administrative expertise were the hated Japanese themselves). Perhaps the United States Army of occupation should have handed authority over to the people and just let them get on with it. But their efforts were vitiated by the growing conviction that Communist Russia, or possibly China, had intentions on the ideological conversion of the people—a view that was by no means without foundation. The Americans were obsessed with the "domino theory" of Communist expansion. The Russians had already had considerable success in creating satellite states in Eastern Europe, and it was now feared that they were about to create further dependencies in the Far East.

As something of a compromise, the country became divided into separate spheres of influence: the North under the despotic Premier Kim Il Sung, and the South under the corrupt regime of American-educated Dr. Syngman Rhee. It was a recipe for disaster (see Hastings 2000). But in the chaotic aftermath of the Second World War, makeshift arrangements were hardly unknown (note the irrational division of Berlin and the calamitous decisions made concerning the Middle East).

The indoctrination of the North had been accomplished in a very short time, and by the high summer of 1950, they were prepared to invade the South. Whether the Soviet regime had actively instigated the invasion, possibly to test the resolve of the West, or whether they had just given the North Korean government the nod, is still not quite certain. Certainly Kim Il Sung would not have made his move without some sort of Russian approval. Support from either the Soviets or the Maoist Chinese (who were soon to be at loggerheads themselves) was essential. Furthermore, the entire venture would have been quite impossible without Russian weaponry; it was Russian armor that carved through the ill-prepared South Korean defense very easily in the initial onslaught.

When the United Nations decided to intervene, it was the United States military who bore the brunt of the attack. They found that the North Koreans who came in wave after wave seemed quite indifferent to life. (It is estimated that they suffered some fifty-eight thousand casualties in the first six weeks of the war.) United States Army veterans had not encountered such unnerving fanaticism since their experiences against the Japanese. The same sort of reckless behavior was exhibited by Chinese troops when it was decided that they should come to the aid of their North Korean allies. Their commanders sent them in en masse with little regard for casualties.

Complementarily, the North Korean People's Army took a similar view of their enemies. Life was held very cheaply. Groups of American prisoners were found shot dead by the roadside. But this was minimal compared with the hundreds of their own people whom they massacred in South Korea during their few months of occupation. It must be said, however, that the South Koreans were not that much better when they had the chance. It was a pointless, fruitless war, initiated for what were ostensibly ideological reasons, which ultimately achieved very little and in which Korea as a whole probably lost at least a million people.

A very similar situation can be found in both Vietnam and Cambodia (Kampuchea). The Indochina Communist Party (ICP) was founded in Hong Kong in 1930. Its leader, Ho Chi Minh, with the patronage of the much more powerful Maoist movement in China, gradually wrested control from the French, who had again taken over the country (now re-named Vietnam) after the defeat of the Japanese in 1945. Somewhat like Korea, the country was divided along political-cum-ideological lines.

The Chinese had plans for their allies, the North Vietnamese, and for their counterpart in South Vietnam, the guerrilla army of the Vietcong, as well as for Cambodia. The Americans, who had become the self-appointed "world's policemen," almost certainly were mistaken in thinking that the Chinese were using their satellites as pawns in a much larger game, whereas the satellite leaders had ideas of their own. However, the Chinese, by building an empire in the Far East, felt that they could embarrass the Americans and challenge Russia's claim to be *the* world's leading Communist state. And the Americans presumably hypothesized that they could "contain" China by encouraging the enmity that existed between them. (This is all rather ironic when one considers that it was the Americans who only a few years before, in 1943, had argued vigorously that China, then an ally, should be admitted to the Conference Table with the other Great Powers.)

From 1954 onward, the whole situation became confused, not to say unpleasant. In that year, the French were worsted by Communist forces (the term "defeat" is often used, but actually the French—a much superior power militarily—decided that it just wasn't worth the agony. As with the Americans who faced a similar problem in

Vietnam a few years later, a cost-benefit analysis of the situation dic-
tated a discreet—if somewhat ignominious—withdrawal).

The North Vietnamese infiltrated cadres into the South from at
least 1960, and the Americans countered with "advisers" to help the
South Vietnamese government. This escalated into a shooting war
by 1962, and in 1964 the Americans initiated a new and far more
dangerous phase by commencing bombing operations in the North.
By 1970 fighting had extended to Cambodia. Casualties mounted on
both sides, and it is arguable that the deadlock could have been broken with the defeat of the North's forces if the Americans had invaded Laos and cut the Ho Chi Minh trail which the North
Vietnamese used as their supply route. The South Vietnamese,
America's allies, greatly antagonized the Cambodians by a "frenzy
of raping and looting" in the villages (Ablin and Hood 1987, xxv).
And this, plus the unwelcome appearance of Western troops, hard-
ened Cambodian attitudes and indirectly facilitated the growth of
the soon-to-be notorious Khmer Rouge, who proved to be far worse
to their own people than the South Vietnamese. In 1970, the Khmer
Rouge had probably at most a thousand troops; by 1973 they had
little short of forty thousand.

The war was prosecuted with great skill by the North Vietnamese,
especially considering their limited resources. But it was also prosecuted with considerable and needless cruelty on both sides. It is estimated that the United States spent the best part of seven billion
dollars on the bombing campaign against a largely defenseless population—something that has since been severely criticized. But what
tends to be overlooked—at least, in some mitigation—is that in the
aftermath of the war, the Americans supplied humanitarian aid to
the Far East in general to the tune of five hundred billion dollars. It
should also be noted that, quite apart from the atrocities committed
by both the South and principally North Vietnamese, some fifty
thousand North Vietnamese had already been "purged" by Ho Chi
Minh, despite the protests of his most able military commander,
General Giap.

This mindless inquisitorial purification of the system is something
we will find again and again, particularly among fanatical ideologues. And no ideologues come more fanatical than Pol Pot, leader
of the Khmer Rouge. Although equally anti-American, the Cambodian Khmers—whose natural ally should have been the North Vietnamese—pursued their own independent, eccentric line. So much
so, in fact, that it was the Vietnamese who eventually had to inter-

vene to curb Khmer excesses against their own people. It was the intention of the Khmer ideologues completely to obliterate the past. They intended to telescope in one operation what it had taken the Chinese twenty-five years to accomplish. The crème de la crème of this elite comprised just eight people: five teachers, an economist, a bureaucrat, and a university professor. All these intellectuals were educated in France in the 1950s, where they had enthusiastically imbibed the teachings of the radical left. In Cambodia they had, at last, the chance to put their ideas into practice—a utopian blueprint which would ultimately claim the lives of twenty-five percent of the Cambodian people.

The Khmers inaugurated a program of radical ruralization which brought unimaginable suffering to the Cambodian people. Some three million people were herded into the countryside and forced to work on the land (according to the ideologues' mentor Mao Tse-tung the revolution had to begin with the peasants). It is doubtful if anything quite like it had ever been seen before—not even in China. Class, status and occupation counted for nothing. The process of social transformation meant the complete dismantling of the entire state and its institutions. Most in danger from the Khmer elite were other elites. Intellectuals of any kind were automatically proscribed. Intellectuals ask questions—and questions often imply criticism—so teachers, civil servants, and the like were duly eliminated. So too were those who were considered too ill or too feeble to work, while those who tended the sick—the doctors and nurses—were forced to work as laborers (only about fifty of some five hundred doctors actually survived). Needless to say, hesitancy to comply meant beatings and often death. Undesirables such as beggars and prostitutes were also exterminated—indeed, anyone who was considered a threat to the regime or a burden to the state.

Much of the actual killing was done by adolescent recruits who seemed to need little encouragement from their seniors (NB, the same phenomenon more recently in certain African states such as Sierra Leone). Most poignant of all was the killing of orphan children, often by young girl soldiers, on the basis that one day they might wish to avenge their dead parents. And as a further refinement, pupils were sometimes made to participate in the deaths of their own teachers. Indeed, the death penalty was very liberally applied for even minor infringements of the rules—that is, assuming that everyone knew exactly what the rules were. At times they appear to have been quite arbitrary, and sometimes entire families would be mutilated or killed for inconsequential acts of "disobedience." In all, probably as many as two million people died from starvation, disease, and exhaustion—not to mention execution (Pilger 1989). Thankfully, Pol Pot's vision was never realized. In the ensuing Communist great power game, his China-backed regime was terminated by the Soviet-supported Vietnamese.

If Lenin and Stalin set the style and the pace, and Pol Pot drew the ultimate conclusions, it was the intermediate agency of Mao Tse-tung that showed how a particular version of Marxist ideology could be operationalized. The term "ideology" can be used in two principal senses: as a set of ideas which serves as a guide and impulse to action, and—as in Marxist usage—as a systematic distortion, exaggeration, or simplification which political leaders use to further their own ambitions. As we shall see when we look at religious ideologies, such belief systems may not lend themselves to a greater understanding of social realities. On the contrary, they may actually employ nonrational and emotional symbols to obscure the truth and enhance the interest of the new political elite. There may be some genuine concern for the suffering masses, which—so it is believed—can only be ameliorated by ultimate success in the class struggle. As Lenin put it, "The liberation of the oppressed class is impossible . . . without violent revolution" (1969, 10). Ostensibly, everything must be subordinated to the interests of the proletariat.

But, surprisingly, there is some debate as to exactly what constitutes the proletariat. Or to look at the question another way, where and by whom does the revolution begin? This is the issue that once divided the Communist camp. Received wisdom had it that revolution must begin with the urban (manufacturing) poor; Mao Tse-tung argued that it should start with the rural peasantry. In a very real sense, this is a sterile argument. Because whatever the agency, the process will be initiated and masterminded by the intellectual elite. The "dictatorship of the proletariat" will be something of a myth simply because the elite, acting on behalf of the Party, will instigate and implement the required revolutionary action which will necessarily include dealing with "class enemies."

In order for this to be achieved, certain stages have to be recognized. This does not, however, mean embarking on a series of social improvements. This would be seen as mere piecemeal social engineering. The aim was a complete change in the nature of society. Earlier so-called revolutions (e.g., those resulting from class conflicts in the classical world) were not seen as true revolutions because they did not aim at radical *structural* change. They simply intended reversals in—or modifications of—the current order of society. To put it bluntly, the poor didn't want to do away with poverty—they just didn't want any longer to be poor themselves. So at the lowest level, slavery could stay as an institution as long as the revolutionaries did not become slaves.

Maoist revolutionaries regarded this as mere tinkering with accepted social arrangements. They wanted a complete transformation of the entire social structure, even if it meant a wholesale elimination of their opponents. So they set out to raise class consciousness. This hardly meant convincing the poor that they were poor; the lower classes were only too well aware of their modest position in the social hierarchy. But it did mean assuring those who were members of a "class-in-itself" to become a "class-for-itself," that is to say a previously underprivileged section of the population that could, and should, work in its own class interests.

The means whereby all this can be realized may not, at first, be overtly violent. Infiltration, subversion, proselytization, and reeducation all play their part. They all have their place in the revolutionary struggle. But where violence is regarded as expedient or necessary there will be no hesitation in using it. So the Maoists and those who have emulated them have never been that reluctant to employ violent means to attain their ends. As their mentor once argued, it is absurd for the revolutionary proletariat to renounce revolutionary wars that prove necessary in the interests of socialism (Lenin 1969). Mao even went so far as to insist that war is a "peace-loving act" if it is done in a right cause. This, of course, begs the question of what is and what is not a right cause. Presumably, the answer is whatever best serves the interests of the people—*and* their leaders.

Actually, regardless of Maoist claims, the Chinese contribution to revolutionary doctrine was hardly original, but its adaptation had certain novel features. In a sense, communism first emerged in China as a reaction to the warlordism in the early days of the twentieth century. Local warlords often commanded vast tracts of territory, and their brutality and confiscations brought incalculable misery to the peasants, particularly through starvation. With this breakdown in the very fabric of society, the rise of the Communist movement can be regarded as a welcome and potentially reformative organization. Yet on a more skeptical (and realistic?) analysis, the Communists could be seen as just another band of brigands, posing as the guardians of the people, who were intent on long-term gains of a particular kind. Their goal was not so much material wealth as power—that kind of unambiguous, naked power, underpinned by belief, which commands unquestioning obedience (not that dissimilar from extremist Islam).

The Chinese Communist Party was formally established in 1921. Members soon came into conflict with the Nationalist Party (Kuomintang), which carried out the obligatory purge in 1927. After more vicissitudes, including the Kuomintang's murder of his wife, Mao led a breakaway group of Chinese Communists, which, after the epic—one might almost say legendary—Long March, became the nucleus of the future People's Liberation Army. In the meantime, they had to cope with the predatory incursions of the Japanese besides the increasing hostility of Chiang Kai-shek's Nationalist Party forces. Added to which there was a fearful famine in Honan (1942–43) in which over two million people died. After the defeat of Japan in 1945, the subsequent struggle for power resulted in a Nationalist determination to destroy the Communist menace once and for all (Chiang Kai-shek actually produced a blueprint for extermination called "Manual on Bandit Suppression"). In the battles that followed there were several reversals of fortune before the Communists finally triumphed in 1949. The Nationalists fled to Formosa, and the Communists took over. Reorganization and retaliation were about to begin.

The task of reconstruction was formidable. The Communists set out to industrialize the country in the shortest possible time. This meant that the measures taken by the new regime were necessarily draconian. What the Soviets had done in forty years, the Chinese aimed to do in less than half this time. There was extensive redistribution of land and later the introduction of "collectivization," which effectively meant the reabsorption of peasant lands into a commune system. It was all part of the much-vaunted "great leap forward," but its limited success was only achieved at considerable cost to personal liberty. Landlords, petty capitalists, and "reactionaries" were suppressed. In practice, this meant "reeducated" (e.g., some university teachers were forced to work as laborers) or unceremoniously eliminated. In some areas, the proletariat (effectively, the rural poor) were urged to terrorize and humiliate local landlords who might then be killed or sent to labor camps. Student groups (the "little Red Book" brigade) were also encouraged to join in the proceedings. We cannot be sure just how many were persecuted or killed, but the Party itself admitted that it had "purged" two million people.

This was really all in line with early Leninist teaching about the just fate of "all kinds of harmful insects"; Lenin's own Secret Police (Cheka) carried out a thousand executions a month in 1918–19. This was regarded as a necessary prerequisite for the reconstruction of society. It was a clinical operation. As he so succinctly—and chillingly—put it: "We are not carrying out a war against individuals. We are exterminating the bourgeoisie as a class. . . . The first question we ask is—to what class does he belong, what are his origins, upbringing, education or profession? These questions define the fate of the accused. This is the essence of the Red Terror" (Johnson 1985, 71).

The potency of belief—religious or otherwise—is most evident when intellectualized as ideology. Belief implies the acceptance of propositions or values which by definition are not susceptible of experimental validation. As ideologies, such belief systems define and legitimize moral and intellectual structures. It is at this point, though, that we do not need to be caught up in the confusing generalities which tend to characterize statements about ideology. What we require are some clues not only about the nature of ideology but also how it "works" in particular situations. What is its contribution to the problem of moral evil?

As we have seen, ideologies justify and explain a preferred social order. This social order may already exist or simply be proposed or anticipated, in which case the ideology in question may constitute a believed strategy for its attainment. This, in turn, may involve an emotional appeal which then generates a sense of moral commitment. Armed with these infused ideals, believers are able to interpret the past, explain the present, and anticipate the future. Nowhere can this be seen better than in the multifaceted ideology of Islam.

Islam, which for many devotees appears to be complete and self-sufficient, is—like so many religious systems—fragmented and internally inconsistent. It is purportedly based on "true principles" that are adhered to by the "faithful" and which are not, therefore, open to negotiation. More than most faiths, Islam recognizes a clear dichotomy between the believer and the unbeliever; between the faithful and the infidel.

The closing of ranks among the devotees has been particularly evident since the West's response to the horrendous events of 11 September 2001, when thousands of people were killed in the World Trade Center and at the Pentagon. The consequent deaths of the immediate perpetrators alone demonstrates the potency of the ideology. Here was moral evil masquerading as moral goodness; murder depicted as a religious imperative.

It is, of course, impossible finally to demonstrate a direct correlation between a belief system and any social form or pattern of behavior. Tests of validity are difficult; thus any hypothesis can at best, never be more than persuasive. A comparative examination shows that similar societies often generate a quite dissimilar range of practices, whereas different societies with different ideologies often produce very similar institutions and practices (compare, for example, the—to modern eyes—bizarre practice of human sacrifice in, say, Aztec Mexico and in Punic Carthage two thousand years earlier). If there are any doubts about this, one might compare the Islamic concepts "jihad" (holy war) and "haram" (acts that are forbidden and punishable) and similar ideas entertained by the ancient Israelites, from whom such notions are almost certainly derived.

We could take the earlier example of the Israelites first. Following the exodus from Egypt where they endured some measure of persecution, possibly in the form of enforced labor, they made what they regarded as divinely ordered incursions into Canaan (Palestine). The dates are uncertain, but the series of invastions may well have taken place during a period of some turbulence in the Aegean and the Middle East (1200–1000 BC). The campaigns to conquer Canaan, led initially by Joshua, the successor of Moses, exhibited holy war in its purest form. The warriors had to be ritually cleansed before battle (including a period of sexual abstinence), and after battle—assuming they were victorious—they declared "herem" all that was taken. We read that after the battles for Ai and Bethel, all the "accursed" (literally, separated) living things were put to the sword as a kind of thank-offering for the victory (Joshua 7–9). Similarly during the subsequent period of consolidation, as depicted in the Book of Judges, there were acts of extermination that were justified in religious terms.

Even two hundred years later, during the early Israelite monarchy, we find retribution being exacted against those hostile tribal groups (e.g., the Amalekites) who were reputed to have hindered the "children of Israel" in their attempts to reach and occupy the Promised Land. Saul, the Israelite king, is instructed by the priest Samuel to "defeat Amalek, massacre him and all that belongs to him, do not spare him, slay both men and women, child and infant, ox and sheep, camel and ass . . ." (1 Samuel 15:3). We are further informed that, just for the record, the ever-opportunistic Saul only destroyed the Amalekite king, Agag. But when Samuel heard of it, he personally slaughtered Agag as a religious act (Samuel 15:26). David, Saul's much-revered successor, was just as adept at the extermination game, also—ostensibly—in obedience to what he regarded as divine imperatives. And so the story continues throughout the highly checkered career of early Israel and Judah, despite the admonitions of the more humanely minded prophets.

Judaism has become considerably modified over the years, but its close Semite cousin, Islam, in its more extreme forms, has carried on the tradition. It is singularly ironic that modern fundamentalist Muslims either do not know—or refuse to see—how close these connections are. Jihad and haram are as old as the Judean hills.

If we glance briefly at the Islamic tradition, we find all the necessary ingredients for the modern spate of brutal terrorist outrages. Theoretically, according to the ethical principles culled from the Koran, understanding, clemency, and compassion are high on the agenda. But when these were reduced (or reinterpreted) in terms of practical rules, we find essential duties distinguished from nonessential duties and lawful actions clearly distinguished from unlawful actions, which are therefore liable to be punished. Among the latter are those designated haram. Among a whole array of sins, and greater even than major offences such as murder, fornication, sodomy, and drinking wine is "misbelief"—a denial of the "true faith."

Misbelief merits various interpretations. Numerous Muslim sects which have arisen over the years, most notably the Wahabis and the Sunnis, who also profess to be faithful to the teachings of the Koran, regard other Muslim groups as heretics. For them the duty of the jihad—effectively an outworking of what is or is not regarded as haram—is obligatory for all Muslims in order to combat the influence of "unbelievers." Yet even here total destruction of "unbelievers" is not necessarily called for. Again, in theory, the injunction is to accept Islam or pay tribute, although some took the ludicrous view that it was to force others to become Muslims, as though one can actually compel belief as opposed to mere nominal submission. In its modern extremist form, this has now become a ritual obligation to exterminate the unbeliever—an obligation that also has ulterior, political overtones.

The Muslims were not alone in this. The Crusaders of the Middle

Ages took a very similar view, supported—needless to say—by the edicts of the medieval Church. Ostensibly the Crusades were organized to liberate the "Holy Land" from the "infidel"—the unbeliever—though this time the infidel was someone who did not recognize the "true Church." But here again we must distinguish between different interpretations of the faith. Although there was a nominal adherence to the teachings of the Early Church among the Crusaders, the very idea of persecuting and killing those who did not share your beliefs was at complete variance with those of the early apostles (Carlton 1990, 104). But this did not bother the warrior knights too much. Indeed, it would not be an unwarranted hypothesis to suggest that their true motives were adventure and plunder as much as anything else. This is clearly evidenced by the actions of Reynold of Chatillon who, en route to Palestine, led the Crusaders in the quite unnecesssary invasion of Cyprus. The theory was that churches and clergy were immune. But Reynold, who later became Prince of Antioch, was in no mood to quibble about ecclesiastical niceties. He and his men sacked the island which technically was part of the Byzantine Empire. For three weeks his troops carried out a campaign of pillage, rape, and murder. Chivalry took second place to lust and brutality.

The fate of infidels was to be very similar. At the Council of Clermont in 1095, Pope Urban II said that part of the world was threatened by warlike Turks and Saracens who hoped to possess the rest. This attitude directly derived from prevailing views of Islam as a militant, expansionist faith. And on the evidence, this was not far short of the truth. Yet it must be conceded that there had been cultural contacts between Islam and scholars in the West once those heady days of early Muslim conquest had passed. Even so, with the Crusades, occasioned in part by what the medieval Church regarded as the desecration of the Holy Land, both sides found ample ideological reasons to slaughter one another.

There was undoubtedly an economic dimension to the Crusades. The Islamic Middle East was seen by many in the West as a place of incalculable wealth and exotic delights, besides being a haven of the unconverted. Lesser knights and impecunious adventurers found the prospect of overseas riches both alluring and exciting—although they knew it was all something of a gamble. But what was also important to them, certainly at the inauguration of the First Crusade in 1095, was that Pope Urban had promised them absolution and remission from the penalties of sin. He had enjoined the squabbling states in the West to cease their bickerings and to concentrate on seeking eternal glory in an expedition against the infidel. (What could be closer to the ideology of those Islamic clerics who send—not accompany—young men on their suicide missions? Promises of post-mortal bliss can be very enticing to the "true believer".) Indeed, according to a famous contemporary divine, Bernard of Clarivaux, they were being offered an amazing bargain that they could not afford to miss.

The Muslims had held Jerusalem since 638, but it was not until the depredations of a fanatical caliph in 1009 that the medieval Church became genuinely alarmed. An expedition against the Muslims in Spain had been launched thirty years before the First Crusade, but once the West became really serious, the response was overwhelming. Again one has to take into consideration the enthusiasm for murder by followers as well as leaders. In one of the early sieges, for instance, at the Muslim-dominated city of Antioch, non-Muslim citizens (mainly Greeks and Armenians) were only too willing to join in the massacre in which no one was spared. In the conquest of Jerusalem in 1099, the Crusaders excelled themselves. They killed every man, woman, and child they could find. The frightful carnage went on unremittingly throughout the day and night. No one was exempt. Even some Jews were herded into a synagogue and burned alive. The only survivors were the governor and his bodyguard, who paid the Crusaders a huge bribe to let them live. It seems incomprehensible that the Crusaders could then assemble for the appropriate rituals to give thanks for their victory. Moral evil was thus sanctified as moral good.

The First Crusade was followed by the Second in 1146, largely initiated by the fervent advocacy of Bernard of Clairvaux. This followed much the same pattern of indiscriminate killing and petered out after two years amid arguments and recriminations among the participants (Oldenbourg 1966). The Third and most famous of the Crusades was launched just a few years later. This had an all-star cast, including Philip Augustus of France, Richard I (the "Lionheart"), and the Saracen leader Saladin. The English king (who was hardly ever in his kingdom) was a man of considerable prowess but already had a somewhat blemished reputation from his wars in France, where English possessions were forever in dispute. Saladin, on the other hand, has mistakenly been portrayed in popular history as a warrior of skill and integrity. It should therefore be pointed out that this honorable man secured his place in the Muslim world by deceit and murder and, though sometimes merciful to enemies, saw fit to kill all the Hospitallers and Knights Templar who were captured during his victory against the Crusaders at Hattin. He is said to have watched with joy because he saw it as an act of purification.

The war was fought with great ferocity (Payne 1994), and the victories were marked by massacre and counter-massacre. Richard, who was said to be a man of some sensitivity and artistic accomplishment, was also known for his policy of blinding and drowning "rebels" in France. At the siege of Acre he surpassed himself. He had three thousand prisoners butchered by men who are said to have relished the prospect as an act of well-deserved revenge. Yet after all this reciprocal slaughter nothing was achieved.

More Crusades followed and were equally ineffective. Ultimately even the Papacy began to despair, even though sporadic hostilities continued. Finally in the thirteenth century ideological considerations began to break down, and we have the irony of Muslim Turks ousting Muslim Saracens and the Church-inspired armies in league with pagan Mongols in an effort to neutralize Muslim power, which culminated in the destruction of the Abbasid Caliphate in Baghdad and the general massacre of its inhabitants.

The Crusades are a study in ambiguity. They were undertaken for a mixture of motives, noble and otherwise. There was no serious attempt to convert the infidel. The Crusades merely demonstrate that greed and glory make a potent combination. And what could be better than eternal bliss as an added incentive?

# Excursus

USUALLY IT IS INFAMOUSLY DIFFICULT TO APPORTION PRAISE AND BLAME when it comes to the rights and wrongs of war. The contending parties all think they have a case. Even outright belligerency is almost invariably justified by a "cause," no matter how spurious. After all, if one does not exist, it can always be manufactured for justificatory purposes. Indeed, it is noteworthy that, in the modern world, the most notoriously aggressive regimes have seen fit to defend their actions in the face of international opinion.

However, having said this, there are instances where the claims of the opposing camps are reasonably unequivocal. The Second World War is a case in point. Even that archpacifist Bertrand Russell, who was imprisoned for his heterodox opinions during the First World War, called its sequel a "crusade." He had no doubts that the Allied cause was just and that the evil of Nazism had to be rooted out and destroyed. But in doing so, did the Allies forfeit the moral high ground?

How justified was the policy of "carpet bombing" German towns on the basis that in "total war" *all* are culpable? And what of German's equally ruthless Tripartite partners who sometimes tend to get left out of the equation? Can proponents justify the dropping of the Hiroshima bomb, which reputedly killed eighty thousand people outright (with a further ten thousand missing), injured thirty-seven thousand, and left many more to die of radiation sickness? And if this can be justified in terms of saving the countless lives of both Japanese and Americans that an invasion of the Japanese mainland would have entailed (the US military estimated about one million American casualties), can we explain the dropping of a second bomb three days later on Nagasaki killing another forty thousand civilians? The view at the time was that these brutally aggressive regimes were getting what they deserved. How many people today remember the horror of the Japanese prison camps and the atrocities of the notorious "death marches"? And how many know that in August 1945 when the atomic bombs were used, in Japanese-occupied

91

Java alone three hundred thousand civilians and Allied prisoners of war were digging their own graves and awaiting execution when the war ended? As we will see, even today the Japanese are reluctant to admit such facts—and certainly not in their schools. Indeed, the memories of such events are growing dim even in our own schools. Evil in history is no longer a commercial commodity.

We surely must regard war, with all its attendant sufferings, as the most significant manifestation of collective moral evil. If this is the case, it is worth noting that modernity, regardless of its enormous technical advances, has witnessed war at its very worst. Humans may have gained increasing control over the environment, but what of humans' control over themselves? The devastation wrought by war in the twentieth century almost certainly exceeds that of any previous century. If anyone has any doubts about this, consider the statistics for the Second World War alone (Weinberg 1994, 882, 894).

Research indicates that just in the Soviet Union, which bore the main brunt of Nazi aggression, the death toll is certainly in excess of twenty-five million. About one-third of these were military casualties, and the larger proportion—something that tends to be overlooked—were civilian casualties. In China, where the war had been going on for much longer, the casualties—which are much more difficult to assess—probably numbered about fifteen million. (In the rape of Nanking, Japanese troops murdered some two hundred thousand civilians, using both military and civilian prisoners for bayonet practice—something that the Japanese are still reluctant to admit and which is barely mentioned in their history books.) In Poland, some six million people lost their lives; but why did these despised Slavs, who suffered so much at the hands of the Germans, then at the end of the war refuse to admit the repatriation of Polish Jews, whose treatment had been even worse? The Yugoslavs probably lost about two million people, the United Kingdom something short of half a million, and the United States about three hundred thousand. And these figures take no account of the innumerable people who suffered in France, Belgium, Holland, Norway, Czechoslovakia, Denmark (admitted for many years by the Nazis as a "favored nation"), and those areas overrun by the Japanese in the Far East, particularly the Philippines.

On the enemy side, the figures are—ironically—not quite as bad. The casualties for Italy, which changed sides in the middle of the war (1943), are uncertain, as are also those for Germany's allies, Hungary, Finland, Romania, and Bulgaria, though they certainly number many thousands. Germany itself lost about four million and Japan something over two million. It is worth noting that in the last great battle of the war, on and around the island of Okinawa, the total death toll was out of all proportion to the size (and importance?) of the objective. About one hundred thousand Japanese were killed, plus many hundreds of civilians, besides some seventy-five thousand American casualties. Perhaps there was some justification in using atomic weapons to end the war, after all. How many more millions would have died attacking and defending the Japanese "home islands" is anybody's guess. (It is estimated that the Japanese still had some seven million troops under arms, including two thousand kamikazi.) It was a genuine "choice-of-evils" problem for the Americans.

As Gerhard Weinberg has so cogently remarked, Germany in particular presented the world with an unprecedented aspect of evil in the deliberate attempt to eliminate physically whole populations from the face of the earth, members of which were to be killed "regardless of age, sex or conduct, but instead solely as a punishment for having been born" (1994, 899). The world still has a problem in comprehending the dangerous capacities of human beings with high levels of education who could both order and carry out such bestial acts (see Carlton 1992 on the Holocaust and the SS Intelligentsia).

# Part II

## The Responses

Since the dawn of history—which presumably means *recorded* history—people have pondered the relationship of the mundane to the supra-mundane. The gods—if they were accepted at all—have always been an enigma. The fundamental questions are perennial. Do the gods exist? And if they do, then do they care? And if they care, why is life so fundamentally tragic, a constant struggle against forces we cannot ultimately control?

But perhaps the gods can be successfully supplicated. Religious systems are predicated on the assumption that the transcendental may have immanental concerns and that there may be methods/techniques whereby such agencies can be harnessed to human needs. Yet are there any clear indications that this is possible? Do prayer, worship, and sacrifice actually *work*? We all appear to be living in an unforgiving cosmos.

Tolstoy (who personalizes the problem) represents what the psychologist of yesteryear, William James, once referred to as the "sick soul," the pessimist (or realist) who sought some meaning to life. He asked, what will be the outcome of my life? Why should I live? Why should I do anything? Is there in life any purpose which the inevitable death that awaits me does not undo and destroy? He confessed that he sought an explanation from "all the branches of knowledge acquired by men," but found nothing, and came to the incontestable conclusion that others who had similarly sought an answer to such questions were similarly disappointed (see Yinger 1957, 406–7).

But, contra William James, is it so sick to ask such questions? At the personal level we all carry the constant burden of disappointment and failure, partly but not entirely defined by society's cultural standards. The wider question of what we see as evil in the world is much more of a problem. This is the central question of religion. It addresses the inevitable tension which arises from the need for some explanation of the mysterious, awesome, and sometimes frightening facts of nature. The cosmic echoes and shadows are a perpetual puzzle to us. Few, if any, human beings have surely been able to avoid such questions. Religion has simply been (as it eventually was for Tolstoy) the attempt to make dreadful things seem less dreadful, the substitution of goals that transcend human experience.

There are various possible modes of orientation to evil and suffering which can be found in both religious and humanistic systems. For those of us who seek explanations, there may be no ultimate answer or, at least, nothing that we can fully understand. For some

intellectuals the problem remains—on their own admission—
unresolved, and there they are content to leave it. This is one aspect
of what the late C. E. M. Joad called "the plight of the intellectual,"
to be beset with doubts and queries that permit of no satisfactory
answers (1951). But there are approaches that we can make—
tentative responses that have been given by those who have been virtually possessed by the problem.

There are a number of ways in which these responses can be categorized. The scheme adopted here, therefore, is just one of many
possible schemes but has the logic of looking at the problem in
terms of certain key academic disciplines. Impressionistically, it may
be thought that this issue is strictly the preserve of theology—which
some may regard as a non-discipline—and more particularly the
philosophy of religion. But I am also including some views offered
by social scientists, as well as considering some neo-evolutionary
ideas deriving from the physical sciences.

# 5

# The Theological Arguments

THE ULTIMATE THEOLOGICAL POSITION THAT REALLY ADMITS OF NO DIS-cussion is that which derives from the Book of Job. In effect it is a form of closure because it maintains that humans are puny creatures with tiny intellects who should not presume to question the divine order of things. Job is taken to task for his temerity and challenged with the unanswerable question, "Where were you when I laid out the Earth and set its boundaries?" Job is silenced. And the lesson for all subsequent enquirers is simply that these matters are not for us and that we should be content with the assurance that omnipotence knows best.

This classic supernaturalistic view of the divine, especially as conceived by the monotheistic faiths, presents real difficulties. On this view, the divine is seen as infinite, all-powerful, and omniscient, who has programmed the world from all eternity and peopled the world with those who—knowingly or otherwise—are here to carry out or comply with the divine agenda. But it is a view that is fraught with problems. Perplexity—indeed, anxiety for the believer—arises from the fact that the divine becomes the creator of both good and evil—a belief that is found most notably in both conventional Judaism and Islam.

But for the believer who does not want to accept such inconsistency there is a real dilemma. This was highlighted for me when I asked an earnest churchgoing friend how he accounted for the Holocaust in religious terms. He was a genuinely caring nonconformist, but his particular theology forced him into a deterministic mode. Puzzled, he could only reply that there must have been something about the Jews that caused God to allow such an unbelievable tragedy. I sensed that it was something he didn't want to say, but given his understanding of religion, it was a conclusion he couldn't very well avoid. I have often wondered just how many well-meaning peo-

ple (including Jewish people, whose intellectuals also have no satisfactory answers) have been tempted to think the same way.

If the cosmos is a divine conception, and the world as we know it
is but one expression of that conception, then what we regard as
good and evil must be facets of that original conception. Therefore
if causality rests with God, then believers are forced to think the un-
thinkable. The conclusion that both evil and good are part of the
divine initiative has to raise doubts as to God's perfection and moral
integrity. To personalize the problem once again: I recall many years
ago speaking to a woman who had been bedridden for fifteen years
and who had been told by some of her friends that she must have
been very wicked for God to punish her in this way. I couldn't have
punished her so and presumably neither could most other human
beings—ergo, does this make me more moral than God? It seems to
be an inescapable dilemma.

We will see from the ways in which believers have tried to cope
with this problem that there is no simple solution, if, indeed, there
is a solution at all. Various intellectual strategems have been tried,
from the view that evil is really good in disguise (i.e., it is a character-
building expedient), to the nihilistic view that evil is purely illusory.
Sandwiched between these we will find the pantheistic view which,
if it accepts the notion of God at all, insists that omnipotence does
not have to imply omnicausality. Thus there is no necessary divine
commitment to the active promotion of what we call "good" and
"evil." This is yet another version of the "evil-derives-from-human-
free-will" argument, which we will see is only a very partial answer to
our problem. Why? Because so much of the pain and suffering in
the world is not the consequence of human moral perversity, nor
even of human ignorance and stupidity. As we have noted, disease
and natural disaster are equally—if not more—"responsible" for
human suffering. The moral freedom response, though obviously
cogent, just will not do as anything like a satisfactory argument.

It must be reasonable to assume that many people have lost faith
because of their inability to resolve the problem of suffering and
evil. In this sense theodicy becomes a practical problem. Their entire orientation in life is challenged; the problem tears at what Peter
Berger calls the "sacred canopy"—that protective belief system
which informs their very existence. It generates skepticism and thus
dispels—even violates—that comforting sense of untroubled well-
being which the Greek philosophers called ataraxia.

As our discussion proceeds, we will find that the history of attempts to deal with the problem—especially in philosophical terms—tends to center on the redefinition, modification, and reinterpretation of already well-rehearsed ideas. But it is difficult to avoid the suspicion that at times this exercise is little more than semantic contortionism. It is surely a form of evasion to suggest, as one modern writer, that the "basic distinction between real and apparent, and between remediable and irremediable evils are for all practical purposes more important in responding to evil than theoretical categories like 'moral' and 'natural' evil." Would we really do better to avoid the "confusion and despair arising from the fact of evils" and see them as "objects of practical concern—ritual, ethical, communal (and) political"? And will we learn more if "we pose the answerable question of why evil was constructed as a philosophical problem . . . rather than pursuing unanswerable question(s) . . ."? (Larrimore 2001, xvii–xviii).

Is this "redefinition" approach really just a way of evading the real issue? Let us restate the problem. Is there any way in which divine benevolence, omnipotence and omniscience can be reconciled with human suffering and the fragility of the created world? And does this dilemma have to lead to atheism? Or can it just remain unresolved as an interesting philosophical puzzle?

As far as documentary evidence goes, the earliest references to the problem go back to Epicurus and his school dating from the fourth century BC. There are further hints in Plato's *Timaeus* (41–42), also in the fourth century BC, where he speaks through his characters of the way in which the created world is a combination of necessity and mind. Here Plato suggests that Mind is the ruling power, and necessity—implying also the presence of suffering—is there to bring about Mind's intended purposes. Although formally articulated by philosophers, the essence of the problem must have been discussed long before this. Indeed, the very fact that people have spent so much time in ritual observances from time immemorial in order to placate the gods and seek their favor indicates a similar sentiment. In fact, it could be argued that all religions in their various ways are systematic attempts to deal with the possible implications of the problem.

The problem was certainly an issue in the early church, and was explicitly elaborated in the second century AD by Marcion, who proposed a resolution of the problem in terms of dualism, i.e., the coexisting presence of two opposing deities representing good and evil. These views were later elaborated by the Gnostic sect which he founded and which was soon castigated as a form of heresy. Gnosticism itself took many forms and seems to have found a favorite breeding ground in Alexandria, then well known as a seat of learning. In general, the main tenets of their teaching was that there was a Supreme Being but the material world was essentially evil and was created by a lesser divinity. It was thus to be despised, and believers were enjoined—somewhat like the earlier Jewish Essene movement—to lead separated and ascetic lives. These views we will encounter again in Manicheanism, which in a later form was rigorously and brutally persecuted in medieval Europe by the Church of Rome (Oldenburg 1961).

The issue was taken up by some of the most important thinkers of the early church. Irenaeus, who became "Bishop" (at that time called "episcopos," literally "overseer") of Lyons in AD 178, attempted to solve the problem in terms that echo Plato and have been recast by modern theologian John Hick. For Irenaeus, evil is necessary as part of the process of "soul-making." In other words, suffering—or more accurately the human *response* to suffering—has an important character-building potential. (Suffering, per se, really does nothing for you. As one cynic once said, "All the world can go to hell when you've got a migraine".) Irenaeus was no stranger to suffering. According to tradition, he died as a martyr (literally "a witness") in AD 202 in the wake of the recent persecutions of believers by the philosopher-emperor Marcus Aurelius and his dissolute son Commodus.

Similar concerns characterized the teachings of the philosopher, Plotinus, who although born in Egypt (circa AD 204) spent much of his time lecturing in Rome. He, too, was greatly influenced by the work of Plato, and it is said that he would have liked to help create a society along the lines of Plato's theoretical blueprint elaborated in the *Republic*. Plotinus also espoused a kind of dualism and maintained that humans "inhabited" two worlds, the World of Pure Intelligence and the World of Sense. And he further argued that only through virtuous living, involving purification, meditation, and self-denial, could mortals possibly attain true spirituality.

By far the most influential of the thinkers of the Early Church who addressed the problem of theodicy was Augustine, who was born in Numidia (modern Algeria) in AD 354. He was the son of a Roman magistrate and was the citizen of an Empire which, though in decline, had "nationalized" the church (a tragedy in the eyes of some dissenting skeptics) and in which its persecution had therefore virtually ceased. In his early years, he was greatly impressed by dualistic arguments which he felt were the only persuasive explanations for the antinomies of human existence. But after some disappointing discussions with Faustus, the leader of what was effectively a Manichean-type sect, he left to become a lecturer. He first taught in Carthage (rebuilt after the almost complete destruction of the city by the Romans during the last of the Punic Wars in 146 BC) and then in Milan. There he came under the influence of Ambrose, the local bishop (later to be regarded as a Father of the Church), and was subsequently baptized.

On returning to Africa, he was ordained and became assistant to the bishop of Hippo (modern Boma), and later wrote his famous *Confessions* (a particularly revealing spiritual autobiography) and the even more notable *City of God*, completed circa AD 426. This optimistic treatise was penned during the disastrous circumstances in which the crumbling Empire now found itself. Rome had fallen to the barbarian hordes in AD 410—a situation that some contemporaries attributed to the benign principles of the "new religion."

Augustine's reputation rests not only on his literary works but also on the battle he waged unceasingly against what he saw as insidious heresies that were undermining the faith. Besides his polemical assaults on the Carthaginian sect of Donatus, who insisted on severe treatment for lapsed believers, Augustine became a byword for upholding the ultraconservative doctrine of predestination, his chief opponent being Pelagius, possibly a British monk, who denied the doctrine of "original sin," and was subsequently condemned for heresy in Carthage in AD 416. This unrelenting conflict with the Pelagians increasingly confirmed Augustine in the view—later restated in somewhat different forms both by Roman Catholicism and the English Puritans—that the world is lost (clearly a Manichean influence) and that there is no salvation outside the Church.

Looked at in this particular way, this is one "answer" to the problem of theodicy because it posits differential treatment for believers and nonbelievers, for the "saved" and the "lost." Augustine, somewhat like modern "crisis (literally, judgement) theologians" such as Karl Barth and Emil Brunner, took the view that without conversion, the individual is incapable of seeing the situation correctly. Sin blinds the unconverted to the nature of evil. The individual is subject to distorted thinking until the truth is "revealed." And revelation comes either via therapy or acceptance of the appropriate ideology.

It is just here that we must lay to rest a prevalent and somewhat insidious academic myth, namely that the problem of evil is essentially a modern phenomenon. This argument derives—understandably—from the fact that with the rise and efficacy of modern medicine and the alleviation, in the West at least, of some of the most undesirable social conditions, humans have distanced themselves from suffering as a "natural" feature of life. The assumption is that once there was an everyday acceptance of pain and death. Such things were completely unavoidable. Hence evil was not a "problem," nor was it *seen* as a problem.

Few would surely contest that industrialization has brought incomparable benefits to the world. Despite the reservations that environmentalists and others are keen to reiterate, generally speaking, people *are* better housed, better educated, and better medicated than in the prescientific world. Though whether we can say with the late Ernest Gellner that industrialization was the "turning point of history" (1963) is open to some dispute. Industrialization—indeed, scientific advance generally—is not an unmixed blessing, but, as the man said, next time you have a toothache, ask yourself if you'd rather live in the Egyptian Middle Kingdom or even in medieval Europe. Can we therefore assume that those who lived in those prescientific times were oblivious to the issue of evil as *a problem*? Odo Marquard obviously seems to think so. He hypothesizes that such people were primarily concerned with the everyday issue of how to survive. "How can I reach next year, the next day, the next hour? In the face of this question, theodicy is not an issue. . . . Only when the direct pressure of suffering and compassion relents, under conditions of distance, do we arrive at theodicy . . ." (quoted by Larrimore 2001, xxix).

In other words, the problem only becomes acute when suffering is no longer a necessary (i.e., unavoidable) part of life. But are the experience and the formulation of the problem mutually exclusive? The problem may not have been articulated or analyzed in any very sophisticated sense in prescientific cultures, but it was surely there, nevertheless? As we have seen, this is really what such religious overtures as prayer, oblations, offerings, and sacrifice are all about. They are a tacit recognition of the problem.

The superstitious awe of the gods in earlier cultures has been well-documented, as is also their oft-acknowledged capriciousness—both indications that evil, however it is defined, is not a new problem. Somewhat earlier in our discussion I mentioned briefly the campaigns of Alexander, and it is instructive that, during his infamous plunder of Tyre, the city's priests chained their idols to the altar lest the gods desert them. Or again, when the Romans threatened the destruction of Carthage during the Punic Wars (264–146 BC) the priests, according to the historian Diodorus, demanded the children of the aristocracy for sacrifice. In giving them up as victims of Melkart, their parents were typically trying to reconcile contradictory values. The divinities gave, but they also took away. Why should this be? It surely cannot be correct to insist that *only* in the modern world has theodicy become both possible and necessary.

Larrimore (2001, xxiv) has written of the too-easy breakdown of evils into "moral" and "natural." But how else is it to be done, unless we indulge in the evasive word games adopted by some modern philosophers? It is therefore instructive to look at the attempts of theologians to systematize their thoughts on the subject. Their ideas—perhaps inevitably—fall into two main categories: the *monotheistic*, where one all-powerful creator deity who for quite inscrutable reasons is the author of both good and evil; and its two main variants, the *dualistic*, where, as in Zoroastrianism, two deities are in perpetual conflict, and the *pseudo-dualistic*, where one god has created minor opposing forces who contend for human souls. (Even the theoretically monotheistic Islam has its Devil. His story has a familiar ring. Known in the Koran as Eblis, he is depicted as an angel who refused to do Allah's bidding and was therefore cast out of Paradise and forced to roam the Earth, presumably in search of both allies and victims. Like Satan—literally, the "adversary"—Eblis is thus seen as the personification of evil.)

The Roman writer Lactantius (b. circa AD 240), representing a pre-Augustian position, argued that humans were the summation of divine workmanship and were created with the ability to discern the difference between good and evil which had been "put before them" by God. Those are the two sides of the coin. They are necessary complementary features of existence; one cannot have one without the other. Without the vicissitudes to which humans must respond, there can be no wisdom. And without wisdom there is no virtue.

The complementary view that evil may not exist as a positive or active force but is merely the absence of good is an ingenious attempt to skirt the problem. Again it centers upon the abuse or misuse of human free will but doesn't really tackle the question of why humans are so created that this is an ever-present possibility. Nor, of course, does it get to grips with the problem of natural evil. Again, we perhaps tend to overlook the very obvious fact that all the world's great religions were formulated in a prescientific environment. They are geocentric in outlook and anthropocentric in orientation. They are necessarily characterized by the most primitive cosmology, and their early practitioners cannot therefore have possibly been aware of the implications of a scientific worldview. It has presented real problems for modern theologians who have had to adapt ancient ideas about the created order to modern audiences.

Another theological stratagem for dealing with the problem can be found in the work of a once much-read scholar, Anicius Boethius (b. circa AD 480), a Roman senator. Essentially, Boethius takes a Job-like stance and criticizes those who out of ignorance think the created order is unplanned and chaotic. Instead, he insists that the world is governed benevolently and that consequently all that happens—no matter how incomprehensible to mortals—is for some good purpose. He even argues that evil exists as a lesson to evil men that they should, in future, learn to be good—a view that skeptics will see as the height of optimism. He even goes so far as to suggest that if only humans could see the eternal plan, they would see that there is a very real sense in which evil is a human perception. It does not actually exist in the economy of God. Some modern writers have taken a similar stance. One of London's most famous preachers, Leslie Weatherhead, used the analogy of the Persian carpet which when looked at from the reverse (wrong) side looked like an incoherent jumble of threads, but when looked at from the right side the pattern (purpose) became abundantly clear. The implication, of course, was that in a post-mortal state what for humans was once incomprehensible will be seen to have a clear meaning.

A very different treatment of the same theme can be found in the work of the American writer Thornton Wilder. In his book, *The Bridge of San Luis Rey*, Wilder takes an actual incident in which five people perished while traversing a bridge that then collapsed. Around this tragic, seemingly inexplicable event, he weaves a teleological plot. Why *these* people? Why were they travelling that way? What were their individual stories? Was there any conceivable purpose in their deaths? Could it have been for some ultimately good purpose?

One of the most famous of the medieval scholastics, Anselm (b. 1033), one-time Archbishop of Canterbury, believed that what he felt to be theological truths could be verified by rational argument.

If this was so, was there not a rational justification for the presence of evil? And if so was the problem of theodicy really a false problem? Anselm offers us an ontological argument. Evil exists because we conceive it to exist. Evil is not simply the absence of good. It is real because we can conceive it to be real. How valid is this kind of supposition? Real as evil may be, it is patently an unsafe argument. The existentialist thinker Jean-Paul Sartre mocks the ontological argument by pointing out how we can conceive of unicorns but there is not a shred of evidence to suggest that such creatures exist or have ever existed.

These early theologians will no doubt be considered hopelessly out of date by some, but even a superficial reading of their ideas is enough to demonstrate how such ideas are clear anticipations of those found in modern writers. So if we take Anselm's argument about the ultimacy of the will in determining human behavior, we find early hints of ideas later elaborated by, among others, philosopher John Hospers. Anselm argued that people choose good or evil because they decide to do so. If we ask the question: why do people make such choices, Anselm is content simply to say that they do so because they *will* to do so. There can be no argument beyond this; will is its own efficient cause. Hospers argued similarly. It is usually possible to address several necessary (contributory) causes for any particular behavioral act or effect, but there will always be one significant "extra" cause, the human desire to do so. It is not a satisfactory argument; for if we ask in that awkward child-wants-to-know fashion why do people will what they will, we are really stuck with an infinite regression.

Even the person reputed to be the greatest of the scholastic theologian-philosophers, Thomas Aquinas, gets us no further, arguing as he did that good was possible without evil. The Italian Aquinas (b. circa 1225) was neither a linguist nor a historian and was a firm believer in the union of state and church. He was a member of that highly questionable order founded by Dominic, a Spanish monk who was canonized (AD 1234) in part in recognition of his bloody crusade against the Albigenses. It was Dominic who initiated the brutal and misconceived Inquisition in which countless people died. It is, admittedly, parenthetical to our main discussion, but it is worth noting that this ostensibly "holy" institution was set up originally in 1229 to extirpate all heresy—or what the Roman Catholic Church regarded as heresy—and was not actually abolished until early in the nineteenth century. Its dealings—one might almost say, crimes—

have never been officially or convincingly repudiated and may well be classified as moral evil in spiritual guise. And this was supported, at least passively, by Aquinas, who held to the twin principles of Reason and Revelation.

These limited approaches to the problem of theodicy can also be found among Protestant theologians. Martin Luther (b. 1483) is still regarded as the founder of the Protestant movement, regardless of the fact that his ideas were largely anticipated by forerunners such as John Wycliffe (b. 1320) and the Bohemian John Huss (b. 1369) (Both were harshly dealt with by the Church Council of Constance in 1415. Their views were condemned; Wycliffe's remains were dug up and burned, and Huss—having been guaranteed immunity—was burned alive and his ashes thrown into the Rhine.) If anything, Luther, once an Augustinian monk, was the *promoter* of Protestantism. Like Wycliffe and Huss, he criticized papal abuses, and, in his case, succeeded in withstanding the power of the Roman Catholic Church largely because he had the backing of certain German princes who also wanted to free themselves from the tutelage of Rome.

Luther also took refuge in the inscrutability of the divine purposes. Humans are in no position to question God's ways. They should adopt an un-Promethian stance, and recognize that heaven knows best. In this he was followed by the greatest of the post-medieval theologians, John Calvin, a French Protestant (b. 1509) who spent much of his life in Geneva. There he was able to set up a theocratic—some ventured to say despotic—government, which ordered the lives of its citizens in minute detail. He is said to have been the most formidable intellectual of the Reformation, and he published his influential theological treatises while still only in his twenties. His intolerance, however (not that dissimilar from Luther's), was starkly demonstrated in his attitude to "heresy." In the condemnation and burning of Michael Servetus in 1553, he displayed much the same bigotry as the Papacy. Servetus, also a theologian and a physician, had rejected the teachings of both Catholicism and Calvinism, and had effectively espoused the radical views of an Italian, Faustus Socinus (Sozini) whose anti-Trinitarianism was later seen to be the seedbed of modern Unitarianism.

Calvin's ideas gave rise to the Infralapsarian movement, which held, like Augustine, that God had created the world for his own glory and had permitted the self-induced "fall of man." However, as an act of grace, God had elected a certain—though indefinite—

number to be saved, while the remainder were condemned to eternal punishment. The more extreme variant was supralapsarianism, which maintained that God had preordained "*before* the Fall" that some people should be saved and the others damned—a view that effectively makes evil a divine creation.

This is, of course, an artificial dichotomy that is still not recognized by many believers of different religious persuasions. To permit is really to ordain, because to decide to permit is to ordain to permit. They are really the same thing. This artificial distinction between God's directive and permissive will is really a theological contrivance to get around the problem of theodicy. It may have an initial plausibility, but it just won't do. It really explains nothing and in its Infralapsarian form quite rules out the theological sine qua non of divine omniscience.

What we have here is unadorned Electionism, which in its best-known forms involves the prescription of external bliss for some and eternal hell for others. (This may be mitigated in Hinduism by a reincarnation process, or in Catholicism by a spell in Purgatory, both of which are calculated to take the edge off the notion of eternal punishment.) Another escape route is possible if we redefine the term "eternal." Should it actually mean "everlasting," or should it rather denote a state of being that is not conditioned by time?

It is ideas of this kind which more than hint at the possibility of divine injustice and have generated the views associated with Universalism. Such ideas can be found in the teachings of Anne Conway (b. 1631), who believed that ultimately all creation would be redeemed, otherwise God would be defeated. These views are echoed in Paul's teachings but were not really developed in institutional terms until the late eighteenth century in the New England states of America. Universalism, which many would like to believe but for which they cannot find any firm justification, is now extremely popular among Unitarians.

Its opposite number, Electionism, still has much support among believers in different religious systems. The "us-and-them" orientation is a legacy of Judaism and its sect-like successor, the Early Church, and can be found today preeminently in Islam. In Britain, it found its fullest development in what is broadly termed Puritanism. Strictly speaking, Puritans were those who refused to accept the Elizabethan settlement of the Church of England and who denounced what they regarded as popish doctrines and ceremonies. They are variously called Dissenters or Non-Conformists and flourished in the mid-seventeenth century, especially during the period of the Civil War. They became associated with "plain living" and strict morality and in general took a categorical view of human depravity and therefore the hopelessness of an unbelieving world.

It is not at all difficult to detect the strong theological connection between Puritanism and Calvinism. Here we have the common doctrine of predestination. The whole world is under condemnation; none are worthy of salvation, all are destined for destruction or unending punishment, but God in his wisdom and mercy has elected that some only should be saved. This is effected by "irresistable grace." No human act or entreaty can bring about salvation; human effort is of no avail. Virtue may be its own reward, but it counts for nothing in the redemption stakes. Salvation is an act of divine grace—a view as much in evidence in modern "crisis" theology as it was in the sixteenth century.

Some may see such views as hopelessly dated, but they are not. Both Universalism and Electionism are still very much with us— albeit in somewhat modified forms. The whole point of this brief review of earlier ideas is simply to show that theologically the problem of theodicy admits of a very limited number of "solutions," all of which have in some way been anticipated by earlier thinkers. No matter which way we look at the problem, we cannot escape the conclusion that if God created the world, he was presumably under no constraint or misapprehension. It is assumed that an all-powerful deity could anticipate what would happen, and could have prevented it simply by not creating it in the first place. So does the buck stop here?

There are attempts by theologians to absolve God of this responsibility. One can argue—unconvincingly—that evil is not God's work because it is alien to his nature. Nevertheless God has called it into existence "not for its own sake . . . but for the sake of the dramatic struggle in which he means to engage with it . . . [a struggle] in which malice is somehow finally cancelled and opposition overcome" (Hodges 1979, 26). We may not detect this design, or see it for what it is, but we are assured that it does exist, and exists for some good purpose.

We could do worse than end this section of our discussion by citing Kant on the pursuit of theology. Kant repudiated the traditional "proofs" for the existence of God (ontological, cosmological, etc.) and argued instead for a belief in a Being who justified the moral life. In other words, he saw moral constraint—the universal sense of "ought"—as being, in itself, a kind of proof of an ultimate Moral Being. It was not possible, he argued, to posit a supreme Being and then deduce our moral obligations from such an initial assumption. Rather, we must reason from rational moral insights to God. Indeed, he once asserted that he was destroying theology in order to make room for religion. One might deduce from his critique of any kind of metaphysical reasoning and our powerlessness to cope with ultimate issues that we should abandon our quest. But there are at least some of us who feel congenitally compelled to go on asking questions.

# 6

# The Philosophical Arguments

THEOLOGY SHADES ALMOST IMPERCEPTIBLY INTO PHILOSOPHY, SO MUCH so, in fact, that the arguments are frequently overlapping and equally equivocal and inconclusive. But they still deserve some consideration.

The problem of theodicy effectively disappears for many modern theologians because they deny the existence of a supernatural deity. (Whether or not they should be called theologians is therefore disputable, although technically the term means examining the logic of the concept "theos/theoi-god/gods"; it does not have to involve belief or religious commitment.) Among those still referred to as the "new theologians," men such as Thomas Altizer, Paul Tillich, and Paul van Buren, supernaturalism as usually conceived is something of an irrelevance. There is therefore no inherent injustice in the order of things. The world is as it is because that is how things are. Theodicy thus becomes a non-problem. Hence the entry of the philosophers, or, in some cases, the philosopher-theologians.

This is not meant to be a quick rundown on the ideas of key thinkers; this can be found in numerous texts that provide readers with essay summaries of great philosophical works from antiquity to modernity. Rather it is an attempt to trace our motto theme with a view to achieving some degree of clarification.

One of the most important philosophical statements on the problem was made by Leibnitz (b. 1646) in his *Theodicy* published in 1710. Leibnitz, together with other continental rationalists such as Descartes and Spinoza, owed much to the classic medieval theologians. He was particularly intrigued by what he saw as the perplexing relationship between God and the natural world, for which he wanted to find a rational solution. In effect, he was trying to resolve the difficulties in reconciling philosophy with theology. In attempting to do so, he adopted a "best of all possible worlds" position involving, as it did, an optimistic view as to the ultimate perfectibility of human nature. For Leibnitz, the divine activity is interventionist activity. God is continually working with his creatures to overcome evil, which he has not ordained but which he has allowed, presumably for the eventual perfection of mortal beings. Logic demands that a perfect divinity would not choose deliberately to create a less-than-perfect world. Thus the world's imperfections—including human imperfections—must exist for some ultimately good purpose.

There are echoes of Leibnitz in his immediate predecessor Spinoza (b. 1632) in so far as both are really saying that if, as they believed, God is a perfect being, then what he has created must be the way it is for good—if often incomprehensible—reasons. In this both Leibnitz and Spinoza are not really taking us beyond Augustine. It is actually the determinist argument all over again. If something *is*, then that is how it was meant to be, and it was meant to be how it is because that is how it works best. It is an argument with an annoying circularity that really doesn't get us very far.

Probably few scholars would disagree that Kant (b. 1724) is one of the greatest post-medieval philosophers. However, he didn't please all his contemporaries by trying to reconcile the views of rationalists such as Leibnitz and Descartes with those of empiricists such as Hume and Locke. Radically, Kant argued that human reason alone can never produce convincing "evidence" for the existence of God. The attribution of divine characteristics such as omnipotence, omniscience, etc., also had to be mere speculation. He rejected the well-tried arguments from design and causality and insisted that they simply involved an unwarranted leap from the known to the unknown. Yet he also argued that without concepts—a kind of inner, intuitive knowledge—we are blind (a view later elaborated with great cogency by philosopher of science Karl Popper). Concepts have a constitutive function in scientific investigation because they imply a systematic unity to the world. And it is this pure reason, with its concept of an ordered universe, that suggests a rational, ordering divinity which/who can be apprehended by rational creatures. But how different, essentially, is this from the argument from design? *If* the universe is so rationally ordered, then why have we a problem?

Ludwig Wittgenstein (b. 1889) might well have argued that we have a problem because we are asking the wrong questions. He insisted that the right method of philosophy is to turn all the things that can be said (i.e., substantive issues) over to the scientists who will be able to deal with them, and to point out to those who ask metaphysical questions that what they are asking is meaningless. In the Tractatus (1921) he is effectively saying that philosophy is not so much a guide to truth as a means to clarification. And in a now famous conclusion, he adds—a little cryptically—that whereof one cannot speak, thereof one must be silent. But can we be silent? Of course there are questions that appear to allow no cogent answers, but we ask them just the same.

If then we still insist on seeking truth, which path do we take? Are we justified in following the precepts of Catholic thinkers such as Jacques Maritain, who argues that the highest form of knowledge is suprarational. Can we discern *the* truth only by "mystical theology"—an experience only given to a few? (An idea which, in practice, echoes Henri Bergson's notion that metaphysics involves intuition.) Notoriously, revelatory knowledge tends to vary with the particular tradition concerned. And Catholic mystics are likely to "see" things quite differently even from those within the same religious tradition. In short, mysticism (intuition?) may not be an infallible source of knowledge.

Another approach to the problem can be found in the work of Josiah Royce (b. 1855), a one-time Harvard academic who made much of the idea that the evil of this world is in its incompleteness—the partial fulfillment of its purpose. Thus we judge the world wrongly. The world, like the cosmos generally, is continually changing (implying development) and—as in the philosophy of Teilhard de Chardin—has yet to reach its "Omega Point." Indeed, Royce comes very close to the Cartesian idea that the overwhelming sense of human imperfection is an indication of the reality of divine perfection. This view can be found in a more generalized form in Rudolph Otto's philosophy of religion: when confronted by a sense of "the Holy," mortals become acutely aware of their nothingness. Are they therefore in a position to ask impertinent questions?

In the philosophical-theological tradition, however, there are different interpretations—one might almost say, perceptions—of finitude. The liberal theologian, Paul Tillich (b. 1886), for instance, argued that it arose out of an anxiety at the prospect of "non-being." This anxiety can be "*ontic*," in that it relates to such inevitabilities as fate and death; it can be *moral*, in as much as humans experience guilt and condemnation; and *spiritual*, in that we have a sense of meaninglessness and despair. In the light of such threats, courage is the self-affirmation of one's being. In other words, we all face the problem of doubt and uncertainty in our own way, and one manifestation of courage (in Tillich's sense) is to do this even though we are unable to understand or explain it. For Tillich, then, philosophical-theological enquiry is about the meaning of being. God may not even exist but merely represent our "ultimate concern." Religious symbols need not be true. Historicity may be in question. What matters is that these things are existentially effective. Salvation consists of the human anticipation of successfully confronting one's finiteness.

A diametrically different view was taken by Tillich's contemporaries, the "crisis theologians." Karl Barth (b. 1886) was a one-time pastor who was later exiled by the Nazis when teaching in Bonn, and afterward became a professor at Basle. Barth was an uncompromising Reformation-style theologian who railed very effectively against the liberal tradition in the churches and condemned what he saw as insidious "modernist" teaching. Barth had early support from his fellow Swiss academic, Emil Brunner (b. 1889), though they were to differ somewhat in later years because Brunner, although firmly adhering to the Reformed tradition, tended to take a somewhat more relaxed approach to doctrine in that he was inclined to allow culture a place as a possible source of truth. Both, however, were agreed on fundamentals. They opposed Catholic doctrines emphasizing the infallibility of the Church, and likewise accused liberal Protestantism of departing from the original Kerugma (literally, the "preached thing," i.e., the Apostolic message).

Barth, in particular, considered all natural theology to be a futile exercise and insisted that humans can never come to a knowledge of God by means of rational argument. He is not interested in philosophical justifications for metaphysical "truths." His dogmatique is based entirely on scriptural revelation and the tradition of the believing community. There is no place for rationalistic quibbling. His view is that truth has entered the world and humans ignore it at their peril. For the crisis theologians—as for the atheistic rationalists—the attempt to prove theological or moral truths must end in failure. Both Barth and Brunner would have had no time for moderns like Paul van Buren, who have little time for talk about sin and grace and reduced the supernatural to the ethics of human relationships. Like philosopher Anthony Flew, the radical van Buren has come to regard the principles and assertions of traditional religion as unintelligible, arguing that they no longer make sense to the "common man."

Similar anti-traditional positions have been taken by numerous philosopher-theologians such as John Robinson (1963), Don Cupitt, and—with certain qualifications—John Hick (1977). Even more radical is the "Death of God" advocate Thomas Altizer (1967). Such Nietzschean sentiments were despairingly echoed not long ago by a Marxist intellectual when he said, "God is dead, Marx is dead, and I'm not feeling so well myself."

There is little doubt that such writers have genuine intellectual reservations about traditional religion with its emphasis on supernatural revelation. But it doesn't require much imagination to suppose that underlying their doubts are the apparent inconsistencies inherent in the problem of theodicy. These have led to ongoing reappraisals by both theologians and philosophers who, needless to say, are still in disarray on the issue.

There is general agreement that the theist of whatever religious persuasion is committed to three assertions: (1) God is omnipotent, (2) God is good, and (3) evil exists. Critics retort that all three cannot be taken together, though—as always—much depends on the definition of the terms. For example, does "God is good" also mean "God is just?" If so, must justice also imply discipline and even punishment? After all, the Church has long taught that "those whom God loveth he also chastiseth." Furthermore, it is frequently pointed out that omnipotence does not—indeed, *cannot*—mean the ability to do anything. Can God do contradictory things? Can God deny his own nature?

But having conceded the definitional and conceptual difficulties, the problem still remains. One philosopher has argued that the most plausible defense open to the theist is the contention that pain and disease (what he terms "first order evils") are necessary conditions for the existence of certain sentiments and virtues ("second order goods") such as sympathy, loyalty, courage, etc. But this, in turn, may give rise to undesirable and unjustifiable "second order evils" such as cruelty (Mackie 1971, 92ff.). So why doesn't God make mortals who will only choose what is good? That, reply theists, would be an abrogation of free will. But critics counter, would that be so bad, considering the disasters wrought by human free will?

In theory, of course, God could create humans who have what might be technically termed freedom of choice but whose wills are so divinely influenced or controlled that their volition is effectively violated. This raises the all too frequently asked question, why doesn't God intervene in order to prevent evil actions? For the theist this is not a logical impossibility, but again the prevention of bad choices necessarily curtails much-prized human volition. Patently this whole tortuous argument turns on what is meant by moral choice, indeed, what is meant by morality itself, and whether human conceptions of good and evil apply outside the mundane sphere.

This is the issue raised by language-games-influenced philosopher D. Z. Phillips. Substantially, Phillips is saying that religion is "true," given its own self-assumed parameters and categories of thought. Therefore it is a mistake to think that religion is in need of justification or that it needs to be shown to be intelligible. It is an error to suggest that religion is false or meaningless. It is not falsified (in the Popperian sense) by normal criteria simply because it is not amenable to normally accepted canons of evidentiality. But can such an argument be persuasively sustained? The flaw, as many would see it, is that it makes religions impervious to any kind of criticism. It certainly outlaws any cogent consideration of the problem of theodicy. Religion, if regarded in this way, is no longer answerable to generally acceptable philosophical tests.

Although Phillips has labored long and hard on such arguments in numerous books and articles (1971, 1977, 1993), he comes down eventually in favor of the regulative functions of religion, by which he means the regulation of thought as well as action. This, he says, is really what religion is—or should be—all about. Here Phillips's approach has much in common with Alfred Ayer's view of ethical statements (1946). Ayer, not a linguistic (Wittgensteinian) philosopher but a logical positivist who laid stress on empirical verification, argued, as we have seen, that ethical statements are merely "pseudostatements" and therefore "without meaning." By this he does not imply that they are foolish or false but that they are not, by their very nature, subject to resolution. As with religious propositions—à la Phillips—they are outside the range of normal discourse; they are the subject of their own particular "language-game."

Phillips insists that philosophy should not be reduced to academic speculation that is totally divorced from the realities of life. He maintains that theological disputation simply diverts attention from the real perplexities of living. He argues that we cannot, anyway, infer the existence of God from the nature of the whole world and maintains that such conjecture is barren and pointless because it cannot be determined by philosophical enquiry. In effect, he is saying that a god who is a god is not capable of explanation and cannot, therefore, be said to "exist" in any ordinary sense of the word. God is not subject to moral understanding, and attributes such as omniscience, omnipotence, omnipresence, and certainly "loving" are outside any comprehensible predications. So for Phillips, *believing* is more important than belief, because belief may be based on uncertain or unascertainable evidence, but believing—whether empirically based or not—may give us something to live by. What Phillips appears to be saying is that religious ideas are neither true nor false, neither rational nor irrational; therefore, there is no contradiction between the believer and the unbeliever. Their different perspectives merely represent different universes of meaning. There is no one paradigm of rationality. Furthermore, one may infer that—contra scientific positivism—there is no *dominant* paradigm of rationality. All such paradigms are necessarily complementary.

In his approach to the problem of theodicy, Phillips warns against over-intellectualization, and insists that we must recognize that such matters are beyond human understanding. He argues that trust in a benevolent deity does not have to mean belief in a transcendent power, any more than talk of an afterlife expresses belief in the reality of post-mortal survival. These are simply ways of coping with the many and perplexing vicissitudes of life. As one critic has put it, "Phillips' account of religion allows no place for polemic, for preaching and apologetics, for mission and conversion, and certainly no place for rational argument. He (even) leaves no place for doubt and scepticism among religious believers" (Stanesby 1985, 180). Or, as philosopher Roger Trigg expresses it, "a god's existence may not depend on our ability to conceptualize, [but] from the point of view of relevance to human life, a god about whom nothing can be said is not so much different from no god at all" (1980, 192)—a point that makes the idea, or possibility, of revelation that much more important.

Philosophical arguments can be both subtle and casuistic, depending on whose interests are being served. They can also be arid and evasive, as we have seen from "language-games" debate. It doesn't really come close to those concerns so eloquently expressed by heterodox philosopher Søren Kierkegaard (b. 1813), who was preoccupied by the thought that death (i.e., the anticipation of death) is the most ethically significant uncertainty of life. As a somewhat heretical believer, and an ailing one at that, he felt that death and suffering had to be consciously appropriated. But he was also very aware—as we all are—of the objective fact of suffering and death as a general phenomenon. Everything dies—but why? And does it have to?

The philosopher-theologian John Hick has made two key, if controversial, points on the issue. He concedes the skeptic's contention that this seems not to be the best of all possible worlds. Impressionistically, it certainly appears to be capable of improvement. But, argues Hick, this depends entirely upon the *purpose* for which the world exists. He contends that the world is a "vale of soul making," a place for the development of the "moral personality" which comes about as a free response to environmental challenges and opportunities. It is only in these circumstances that humans can develop those qualities of unselfishness, love, and sacrifice that are so often generated by pain and suffering. We appear to live in an untidy and imperfect world, but these qualities would almost certainly not arise if we had been granted some sort of "hedonistic paradise" (1974, 158).

Hick's position is that evil—a factor of uncertain provenance—is ideally contrary to the divine will, but as a fact of existence can be used to facilitate the ultimate purpose of spiritual growth. This, he maintains, cannot be proved to the atheist's satisfaction. But eventually the believer may be vindicated by what Hick calls "eschatological verification" or post-mortal confirmation—a theory (if it can be called a theory) that even philosopher-theologians have treated with some skepticism. It is hardly evidence for those with genuine intellectual doubts. But what else *can* be said? (I have sometimes mused that on my gravestone—in the unlikely event that I will ever have a gravestone—there could be inscribed the plea, "Perhaps now I'll get some answers.")

The "vale-of-soul-making" response to the problem of theodicy is superficially plausible, but it can never be any more than that. Are we really to suppose that the many travails of life are simply "sent to try us"? What of false starts and mass extinctions? Are plagues that decimate entire populations and wars that successfully eliminate untold millions all part of some deliberate unfathomable divine plan? Surely the price is too high? The combination of a challenging environment and the gift of human free will cannot be worth *that* much. It might be more apposite to speak of a "vale of tears" rather than a "vale of soul-making"!

Another variant of Hick's argument can be found in earlier texts written by extremely concerned and well-meaning academics. Edwin Burtt, referring to the suffering of the Jews, hypothesizes that these "Terrible calamities . . . are not a proof of special guilt on their part but rather a specially exalted role that Yahweh is calling them to fulfill. Hence it is not a sheer evil . . . but an experience that can be turned to a new, hopeful, creative use . . . and can purge them of the proud, self-centered vices that had corrupted them in the past. . . . a necessary preparation for a unique spiritual role." (1957, 327). Similar sentiments can be detected in treatments of the controversial theme of personal sacrifice, which admittedly requires a certain kind of spiritual courage. It is only in this way, according to some theorists, that "biological life [can reach] to a higher order of 'transcendent spirituality'" (Peterson 1972, 176). This is all very reminiscent, yet again, a Teilhard de Chardin (1951), who contends that human life and consciousness may not be the final step in the scale of cosmic evolution but simply an indication of what will one day be possible.

Yet again, the problem remains. Perhaps de Chardin is right; perhaps life is still evolving, and perhaps humanity as we know it is still at a very modest stage of development. But why such a lengthy and costly process? Can the argument from design possibly be sustained? That some element of design is present in creation is something that is conceded even by many skeptics. The notion that everything came about by random chance seems—if anything—more baffling than many theistic orthodoxies (an argument we will consider further in part III). After all, some kind of purpose does seem to be evident in the cosmic world, and it is hard to believe that it is all the result of some stupendous coincidence. The law—if it is a law—of inverse probability would appear to rule out the idea of an unintelligent universe (see Delsemme 2000).

The problem of evil in the world does not abrogate the argument from design, but it obviously qualifies it in important ways. Evil does not seem to be a negative quality—the mere absence of good. The experience of evil does not appear to us as being simply the lack of something in creation, or in society, or even in our lives. Rather it often manifests itself, or is manifested, as a positive quality. It's more than the weeds among the wheat; it is the very presence of the weeds themselves. Why, and for what purpose, do they have to exist? Yet if all creation is benign and purposive, then we seem to be involved in a logical contradiction.

It is, of course, possible to ignore the problem of evil, as per some pragmatist philosophers like Thomas Dewey, and is certainly implicit in the writings of nontheistic existentialist philosophers such as Jean-Paul Sartre. But it is hardly possible to entertain such notions as being "beyond good and evil," in the fashion of Friedrich Nietzsche. The graphic personification of evil in such figures as Satan, Lucifer, Ahriman, et al., crop up regularly in the world's religions as striving to possess mortal souls. Can we take such ideas seriously, or should we suppose that such representations are intended for simple people in earlier times? On the other hand, are they forms in which a metaphysical reality is made comprehensible and therefore believable? Even in systems that are termed religions but which are really humanistic philosophies, such as Confucianism and Buddhism, the tacit recognition of evil is present. Gotama (Buddha) himself taught that unhappiness and despair were the inevitable lot of mortals and could only be conquered by the appropriate degree of discipline and resignation—in effect, by making virtue of necessity. This was hardly a consolation, and certainly not an explanation, but presumably it was better than nothing at all. But then, as Jacques Maritain once self-effacingly pointed out, philosophers play a strange game. They know that the reason for our existence is the only question that really counts, yet it is a question they are never going to be able to answer. Nevertheless, he says, they continue sedately to amuse themselves.

# 7

# The Social Science Arguments

SOCIOLOGY HAS ITS ROOTS IN PHILOSOPHY (THE TERM "SOCIOLOGY" WAS coined by the French theorist Auguste Comte, who originally referred to this form of social enquiry as "the philosophy of society." So it should not be regarded as that unusual that sociologists of religion should be interested in the problem of theodicy.

The seminal work here was done by the German theorist Max Weber, who saw clearly that religious systems had a rational need for a theodicy of suffering and death. His studies showed how evident was the sense of injustice and even resentment, especially on the part of those of the socially disadvantaged strata who saw "the unrighteous prosper as the green bay tree." Consequently, he hypothesized that there are really only three plausible forms of theodicy: (1) *dualism,* which contrasts the powers of good and evil, light and darkness, purity and corruption, etc., which coexist in either permanent or temporary conflict. It can be found in one form or another in several religious systems but classically in Zoroastrianism, in which the forces of light (Ahura-Mazda) are pitted against those of Ahriman, the fount of evil and death. Zoroastrianism, founded probably as early as the sixth century BC, and today represented by Parseeism, maintains that this titanic struggle between these opposing forces must culminate in a victory for Ahura-Mazda, the Supreme Creator, but that it will only be brought about by volitional human cooperation.

A very similar conception can be found in the idea of God versus Satan. But, whatever form it takes, dualism does not really solve the problem. (Even modern Parsees are not happy with this limitation on the power of the Creator.) Dualism, whether in a Manichean or Gnostic form, does not resolve the issue of how an omniscient God cannot forsee the evil that will result from the Evil Spirit who is also part of his creation, nor how this can be squared with assurances of divine love.

But there are compensations. As Weber points out, with special reference to dualism, a theodicy of disprivilege, of whatever kind, is a component of every salvation religion. Privation can be intellectually transmuted into a sense of singularity and self-respect. The Early Church inherited these compensatory ideas, although in this case, the promises did not take the form of ideological justification or of material rewards but of intangible but virtuous spiritual endowments.

Yet, for all this, the problem remains of how—in Weber's terms—the extraordinary power of a transcendental unitary god may be reconciled with the imperfections of the world. He reiterates that theodicy is preeminently a problem for monotheists because where there are many gods, each can represent different aspects of experience—both good and evil. Thus he posits: (2) *polytheism,* as the most complete formal solution to the problem. Here the world is viewed as "a completely connected and self-contained cosmos." In the Hindu doctrine of Karma "guilt and merit . . . are unfailingly compensated by fate in the successive lives of the soul which may be reincarnated several times." In this way, what may be seen as unjust suffering in the terrestrial life can be regarded as a form of atonement for the sins of a previous existence (1966, 145–46). In its Buddhist form (strictly an offshoot of Hinduism), this rather mechanistic view of the eternal order has been developed with particular consistency. In what is effectively a godless system of salvation, it is open to question whether even the soul has been retained in anything like the original sense. An impersonal ego is merely absorbed into the Great All.

Finally, Weber cites: (3) *predestination* as an answer to the problem, although this is really another version of election doctrine. No one merits salvation. The world is really a lost cause. All are under condemnation, yet God in his mercy has decided (for reasons unknown to us) that some shall be saved. The privileged are in no sense worthy of this honor. Their salvation is entirely an act of grace—a view that takes us back to Augustine, the Puritans, and the crisis theologians. This view outlaws the idea of an inexplicable fate and substitutes that of an unfathomable providence. But it cannot avoid the necessity of human renunciation. For what is ordained is ordained. There is no escaping the inscrutable wisdom of divine judgment.

All societies have conceptions of a supernatural order which, in some sense, is thought to be related to, or even to govern, the actual world. This order is rationally impenetrable but may be contacted and placated by a variety of ritual and behavioral imperatives. In institutionalized forms it is known as religion. And it is this analysis of Weber's, from which much subsequent thinking in the sociology of religion derives, which is seen (with minor variations) as the logical resolution to the problem of "meaning." In one way or another, these three "responses" are said to reconcile the inevitable moral discrepancies which arise from the divine will–human condition dilemma.

The predestination argument in particular poses a problem. Indeed, there is a hidden, possibly unperceived, contradiction in the central thesis. If moral evil is an inevitable corollary of human free will, and that free will is a necessary and much-prized component of the human condition, how can this be reconciled with divine ordination, about which elect individuals presumably have little choice? One way round the dilemma is to stress that some human free will is involved in the salvation process, but it is stressed that this is insufficient in and of itself. What is required, according to the Reformed tradition, is "enabling grace." In other words, God facilitates the salvation of the chosen, and without this help they are quite incapable of responding to the divine overtures. Unbelievably privileged as they are, the chosen have not really fully exercised the freedom they have been given.

Sociology together with its close cousin social anthropology has been preeminently concerned with religious ritual. The underlying assumption has been that ritual, unlike beliefs, is something that is amenable to empirical investigation. The tradition stems very much from anthropologists such as Bronislau Malinowski, David Bidney, and Edmund Leach, who felt that ritual is the visible expression of belief. By extention, therefore, ritual is one way of coming to terms with the unwanted and perplexing exigencies of life.

There are many ways in which the functions of ritual can be categorized. Anthony Wallace suggests five ways in which rituals are believed to effect "transformations of state" for the participants (1966, 240–42): (1) as *technology*, i.e., acts such as divination in order to discern the will of the gods, and more specifically sacrifice, which is held to influence the relevant divinities and secure their favor. This can be seen most notably in the supplicative and protective rituals of fertility religions, such as those found in preconquest Mesoamerica. Nowhere else was human sacrifice, in particular, practiced on such a vast scale. For example, at the opening of the pyramid-temple complex of Ahuizotl in Tenochtitlán (modern Mexico City), several thousand people were sacrificed. Indeed, as we have seen, it is believed that the main reason for the predatory wars of the Aztecs was the need to secure captives for the "stone" (i.e., the altar stone over which victims were stretched inorder to extract their hearts as offerings to the gods).

(2) as *therapy*, i.e., as an antidote against evil forces. In practice, this was often meant as a defense against witchcraft or the malevolent actions of "known" and unknown demons that were waiting to bring pain and misfortune. Here we are back with the problem of theodicy. How can people avoid—as they believe—the work of evil agencies? And why are the gods, whom they do their best to placate, prepared to let mortals suffer in this way? Unsophisticated as the preventative rituals often are—and they can include the most superstitious practices, even in modern societies—they are the vain cries of the spiritually impotent. Even the most devout can never guarantee a favorable outcome.

(3) as *ideology* (i.e., codified belief) ritual reaffirms tradition and reinforces faith in the religious system in question. The regularization of ritual procedures and the discipline of devotional exercises involving set reiteration of the requisite creeds, mantras, and religious formulae serve to reconfirm the truths of the system and assure believers of their place in the order of things.

(4) as *salvation*, ritual provides the transformative means whereby the devotee conforms to an idealized image of the "true believer." This may involve much more than the repetition of the prescribed ritual acts; it can involve what some describe as a mystical experience (as some undergoing adult baptism, for example, will testify). Again, such experiences serve to reinforce the tenets of the faith and confirm the participants in their commitment.

(5) as *revitalization*, this is really just another way of expressing the outcome of those rituals which confirm a sense of salvation. Ritual acts—usually in company with others—act as an ongoing encouragement to believers and a fillip to their faith.

These categories/classifications clearly overlap and are fairly typical of sociological/anthropological analyses. But they are broadly useful in that they highlight the ways in which believers seek to ensure that their commitment is "safe," and that regardless of the vagaries of life, there is a point and purpose to their existence. This is the central question of religion. Essentially, life is a mystery. The entire purpose of religion is to reconcile individuals to the awesome facts of the natural world and to the moral incongruities of the social order from which they may feel increasingly alienated. It is in these circumstances that mortals become acutely aware fo their own powerlessness.

Humans everywhere seek gratification, so life becomes a series of adjustments. But frustration and a sense of injustice arise when they endure pain and deprivation unequally and haphazardly. They cannot easily dismiss such things as something which "just happens." They feel compelled to seek answers and to endow the seemingly imexplicable with some kind of meaning. It is for this reason that people resort to religion—to seek a transcendental reference which, they trust, will bring ultimate consolation.

The social scientist, however, wants to know in what kinds of societies the various interpretations of evil arise. Why do certain religions see society as basically "good"—the sort of thing we find in the different manifestations of humanism from Epicurianism onwards? And why do others view society as fundamentally flawed and in serious need of redemption? What is particularly interesting here is that there is no obvious or simple progression from one type to another. The religions, for example, of tribal peoples—despite their often difficult living conditions—do not appear to have been notably "pessimistic" in their view of the world. Indeed—and this is another fascinating anomaly—only some have been obsessed by witch beliefs, a phenomenon that is almost invariably associated with evil. This is similar for ancient religions. All, of course, have their demons and evil spirits, but their worldviews sometimes differed in significant ways. For instance, in ancient Egypt where, broadly speaking, the life-giving Nile inundation was regular and therefore predictable, the gods were generally regarded as either benign or beneficent. This may be contrasted with contemporaneous ancient Mesopotamia, where the Tigris and the Euphrates were subject to inexplicable flooding. Life there was more precarious, and unsurprisingly the gods were regarded as capricious and even malevolent.

Complementarily, soceites that are so organized that aspirations are blocked and poverty and oppression are the order of the day (as, say, in serf-based sixteenth-century Russia) are likely to entertain highly pessimistic conceptions of evil, as, indeed, are those that quite regularly are overwhelmed by pestilence and war. There is no perfect correlation between religious conceptions and levels of suffering, but socioeconomic conditions must inevitably shape the values of members and influence their interpretive approach to good and evil.

It follows, therefore, that theodices will also differ, though the routes to understanding and adjustment will be influenced by similar factors. We may even go further and suggest that conceptions of "salvation" come into a similar—possibly determinative—category. Sociologists of religion tend to cite three ways in which religious systems specify that salvation can be achieved: by action or "works," by devotional rituals (including sacrifice of time and money, etc.), by knowledge (which may be "intuitive," as in Hinduism and Buddhism), or by some combination of these. All are in some way predicated on conceptions of suffering and evil, and the "solution" to the problem is almost invariably seen in transcendental terms. The problem and its answer are relocated to a prospective hereafter.

In modern highly secularized societies, the question of theodicy does not tend to arise in its traditional form, although there is an ultimacy about the problem which cannot be avoided even here. Modern society is more inclined to embrace quasi-religious ideologies such as socialism, nationalism, Marxism, and the like, which act as spiritual surrogates. Or it is content to settle for the accepted certainties of science as the dominant paradigm of our time. These at least bring a transient sense of salvation, but they can hardly bring that more satisfying sense of "wholeness" (the complete or integrated personality) which salvation (in Greek, *sozo*) really means.

A particularly perceptive treatment of the problem can be found in the work of Peter Berger (1969). He stresses the universal nature of the problem and commonsensically maintains that theodicies can be differentiated in terms of their degree of rationality, and here he very much follows Weber's typology. Do they coherently and consistently explain the phenomena in question in terms of an overall view of the universe? Whatever the explanatory system or *nomos*, it comprises for the individual, according to Berger, an all-encompassing universe of meaning. At least, this is the theory. In practice, this fabric of meaning is pierced at various points by doubts and questions. There may, of course, be an ongoing process of denial, an unwillingness to confront the implications of the problem squarely and adopt an attitude of virtuous Job-like resignation. But how long can this submission to the absolute last, when faced with the increasing demands of an insistent and non-masochistic rationality?

Berger is keen to point out that theodicies are primarily about meaning, and not about happiness, although presumably a glimmer of meaning—a feeling that one has got some kind of an answer— must bring a sense of well-being. To this extent they may function as

Marx's "opiate of the people," (though it is important to note that here Marx was being critically sympathetic to religion as a social alleviative). Neither may it have a redemptive character in the religious sense, although it may act as a form of social compensation (though on these issues much would depend on the nature of the theodicy in question). For Berger, the complete subordination of the self (individuality) to the ideology of the collectivity is a stereotypically irrational act. We find this sort of thing in situations where an individual becomes secondarily socialized by a religious or political group with strict, highly codified views. By what sociologists call a process of "self-transcendent participation," bonding can take place within fundamentalist groups of whatever persuasion (Moonies, Scientologists, etc., would be classic examples) and facilitate what amounts to an intellectual transformation. In recent years it has been tragically shown that individuals recruited, for example, by militant Islamic groups can be "given" a worldview that changes their whole moral outlook. Even death and the death of others—especially those regarded as enemies—takes on an entirely new meaning.

This kind of irrational ideology has, paradoxically, its own peculiar rationality. This takes the form of future vindication which may be other-worldly or this-worldly in conception. It may involve a "re-reading" of history to make it consonant with the ideology. The present will be reinterpreted in terms of the past, and the future will be viewed with millenarian anticipation. There may even be an upsurge of revolutionary zeal combined with a hope of divine intervention. The process is seen as inevitable, though perhaps—as with the once-vaunted "classless society"—aided and abetted by a little human assistance. The main problem with this kind of theodicy is that unless redress is located in an other-worldly context, or it is postponed until the distant future (a difficulty that the apostle Paul faced in writing to the church at Thessalonica), it is always liable to empirical disconfirmation. The this-wordly "solution" can, of course, always be transposed to the hereafter, or it can be reinterpreted as a hidden process (e.g., a "Secret Rapture") within the current order.

Sociologists recognize polytheism and dualism as persuasive responses to the problem of theodicy. Yet polytheism poses the initial difficulty of accounting for a mutiplicity of often bizarre and morphologically implausible deities that often vie with each other for precedence and control. Can we really take seriously the Hindu idea of Shiva in his avatar as the cosmic destroyer, or Shiva performing his dance of creation on a mountain of human skulls? Dualism has more to commend it. Straightforward no-nonsense good versus evil has much going for it. Humans participate in this cosmic struggle in which it is believed good will ultimately triumph. In its Gnostic/ Manichean form it is believed that the material world with all its imperfections must be the creation of negative forces. Complementarily, in theory at least, the good divinity cannot be held accountable for its prevailing disorder. But, as we have noted, this does not entirely absolve the good divinity who, for incomprehensible reasons, has allowed—and continues to allow—the current state of affairs to continue.

The predestination argument that we have already encountered in both the theological and philosophical responses, though initially persuasive, actually presents us with insuperable moral difficulties. In its most rigorous—and therefore most extreme form—it is totally uncompromising. In Islamic and Reformed theology, God is the absolute master and judge of the created order. As sovereign power, the deity is beyond questioning; indeed, it is effrontery—even blasphemy—to doubt the divine wisdom. Mortals cannot begin to understand ("My ways are not your ways, saith the Lord"). They should be humbly thankful for what they have been given. But more perplexing is the Calvinist doctrine of arbitrary divine judgment which consigns the non-elect to eternal damnation. As a response to the problem of theodicy, it has its own peculiar—if terrifying—logic. The Calvinistic vision of the condemned and the saved alike glorifying God conjures up images of the Soviet treason trials, in which even the proscribed and their relatives still praised the party and its despotic leader. It is both sinister and revealing that such different conceptions can be so closely associated.

We see, yet again, that none of these responses is ultimately satisfying. Every one leaves us with persistent, unanswered questions. Essentially, "theodicy represents the attempt to make a pact with death. Whatever the fate of any historical religion, or that of religion as such, we can be certain that the necessity of this attempt will persist as long as men die and have to make sense of the fact" (Berger 1969, 80).

Such responses are particularly interesting from a psychological point of view. Scientists tend to regard the concept of "evil" with some skepticism. They are especially suspicious of claims to possession by personified demons, not least because this implies that evil has an objective dimension instead of being a feature of the human personality. Yet such beliefs have been—and still are—common to many religious systems and are held to be responsible for the ills that beset us. Furthermore, apologists who defend the conservative position within such religious systems argue that if such evil personalities did not exist, their sacred traditions would have told them so. And who are they to deny the truths of the scriptures or the wisdom of their holy men?

As a footnote we might add that psychologists are keen to stress the value of "awareness"—something that may be brought about by reeducation or psychotherapy of one kind or another. Awareness, so it is claimed, brings freedom "to follow the voice of reason . . . against the voices of irrational passions" (Fromm, 1964, 131). Here the emphasis is on the necessity to escape from a sense of guilt and oppression (qualities of the "sick soul"), and eschew the morbidity often engendered by a religious outlook. As one critic has commented, "a one-sidedly optimistic religious faith connotes a rather naive suggestibility, predisposed to see religion as a haven by denying the harsher aspects of reality" (Meadow and Kahoe, 1984, 357). The implication is that problems which only bring depression should be studiously avoided. But the problem of theodicy will hardly go away if we just don't look at it. Can we be aware of our failures, and our finitude and let it go at that?

# 8

## The Neo-evolutionary Arguments

EDWARD CRANKSHAW, WRITING OF THE ABUSES CURRENT IN MID-nineteenth century Russia, speaks of those "who seem to find diffi-culty not only in distinguishing between the evils endemic to hu-manity and those arising from a particular and local society but even in realising that such a distinction exists." And adds that the faintest recognition of the existence of original sin as distinct from the sins of the regime would have been a distinct advantage (2000, 225).

The same sort of thing might be said of the social evolutionists who see the prevailing deficiencies in humans as the inevitable con-sequence of mistaken or mismanaged social arrangements. Social evolutionism, deriving as it has from evolutionary theory, has in the past argued that there is a parallel between the general principles of biological evolution and those underlying social change and devel-opment. Adaptation and diversity are obviously common to both bi-ology and society, but whereas biological evolution is—as far as we can tell—unintended and random, social development, by and large, is conscious and purposive. Consequently, social evolutionism (sometimes known as Social Darwinism) has had many critics, espe-cially among those who wish to think of humans as beings who shape their own destinies.

Nevertheless, as a very broadly conceived theory of unilinear de-velopment, it has brought together academics of many persuasions, those of the left (Marx et al.) and those of the right (such as sociolo-gist Talcott Parsons). It also unites those who may be generally classi-fied as believers and those who occupy the well-patronized agnostic fringe. It is argued that any substantive social theory has, in some sense, to be evolutionary because not only are social capacities or-ganically based, they have taken—with some hitches—a generally unilinear direction in which certain elements (institutions and prac-tices) have selected to advantage (Runciman 1989). Whether, of course, one can take the next somewhat uncertain step and speak of

131

social progress is another matter. This implies a "better and better" scenario that is patently open to debate.

A variant of social evolutionism that makes quite different fundamental assumptions is sociobiological theory. Its initial principles do not support the onward and upward unilinearity of social evolutionism. Instead, they tend rather to a deterministic stance and divest humans of their own (and society's) transforming capacities. In short, sociobiology seeks to provide biological explanations for the evolution of human behavior. This view, particularly associated with writers such as Edward Wilson and Richard Dawkins, maintains that there is a biological basis for social action and—by implication—all human values. Even such an apparently selfless value as altruism has an impartial demographic function. It is seen as nature's way of preserving the stability of the group and transmitting desirable genetic material to the next generation.

Needless to say, sociobiological theory has been severely criticized by a number of sociologists, philosophers, and even fellow geneticists for its one-dimensional, rather simplistic view of human behavior. It is argued that such an all-encompassing synthesis takes little account of cultural diversity and is essentially reductionist and determinist in that it leaves little scope for human volition. Nevertheless, it has a certain appeal, especially for those interested in sexual gender roles, though it hasn't gone down too well with homosexuals or with feminists who see it as an insidious support for patriarchy.

It really goes without saying that deterministic theories of this kind share little with those of traditional theology, although theologians whose sympathies are rather more outré would have more in common with the neo-evolutionists. Certainly the so-called "process theologians" and those influenced by the de Chardin school would give more credence to neo-evolutionism, regardless of its unashamed agnostic bent. The more society has moved away from according evil any ontological status, the more the problem has receded into the background. Evil has been increasingly identified with specific undesirable social traits. And this, in turn, has led to some interesting euphemistic evasions. Criminals have now become sociopaths, and sociopathy is spoken of as though it were some kind of disease. Sin, needless to say, is hardly spoken of at all; it tends to be associated with the puritanical mores of nineteenth-century social reformers. It conjures up notions of Bands of Hope, teetotalism, and sexual restraint, which are now seen as entirely outmoded. And the very idea of "original sin" is now so totally passé that it is doubtful whether the general public is even aware of the term, let alone what it means and what it implies.

So does the idea (or concept) of evil have any modern relevance? Not according to some theorists. Consequently, "the problem of evil" is said to be no longer a mystery. Indeed, it is claimed to have been solved by one young parvenu writer in his first book (Anders 1994). What theologians, philosophers, and scientists have pondered for aeons has now yielded to common sense. Previous responses—so it is argued—have been unconvincing and unhelpful. They were based on misconceptions and prejudices. But now we are informed that there is a simple and compelling answer, an "original and persuasive solution . . . that is grounded in science," none other than evolution by natural selection—a theory that is hardly new but that deserves attention.

Neo-evolutionism is yet another form of reductionism. Its basic assumption—some might say its reductio ad absurdum—is that creatures are simply complex agencies for carrying and transmitting microscopic replicating cells. As one theorist graphically suggests, it is comparable to some "mad mechanical genius" constructing a vast, intricate computer in order to do a very simple mathematical calculation.

Somewhat patronizingly, neo-evolutionism derides other attempts to solve the problem of evil simply by arguing that the problem doesn't exist. That is to say, it doesn't exist *as a problem*. What we designate as evil obviously exists: disease and suffering, brutality and oppression—all of which we are only too painfully aware. We live in an unheeding world. But, it is argued, evil only becomes a problem if we entertain the naive view that this is not what was (or is) intended, or if we think that evil has some external, malevolent source. Thus it is a problem for theologians and philosophers who have tried vainly to come up with plausible answers. But it is not a problem for science—at least, not for right-thinking science.

The orientation is not normative but substantive. The neo-evolutionist view is that we live in a world with things as they are rather than things as they ought to be. Utopianism is simply fantasy. The implicit injunction to meta-physicians and sundry theists is to "get real." Anything other than that which is empirically verifiable is probably delusion. Anything other than reality (assuming we know what that is) is mere window dressing.

The problem of evil is therefore said to rest upon a gross misunderstanding. Previous explanations have been based on superstition.

What was required all along was a rational appreciation of the facts. These had been suspected for some time until they were triumphantly verified by Darwin. Yet it is persuasively argued that even Darwin can be misinterpreted. Evil also becomes a problem if philosophers *and* scientists come to see the natural world as benevolent, with evolution working to further human interests. Without this initial presupposition, evil is not a problem, but, as neo-evolutionists readily concede, it is still something of a mystery—that is, unless one is prepared to see the origins of human suffering in terms of an entirely neutral evolutionary process.

A further departure from the theological-philosophical approach is the unwillingness to distinguish between the conventional terms "natural" and "moral" evil. In fact, the distinction is regarded as irrelevant because both natural and moral evil are seen to derive from the same source, the biological capacity for suffering.

Hence in neo-evolutionism lies intellectual emancipation. Yet this "forgive-me-for-being-born" thesis really says very little. Of course, there would be no problem if either (a) humans did not exist or (b) they merely had the intelligence and sensitivity of earthworms and were not therefore aware of their own condition. Even a most elementary knowledge of biology teaches us that, with certain exceptions, suffering serves no long-term useful purpose. It is neither benign nor adaptive. But is the riddle really solved if we can discover what are hypothesized as the "ultimate roots of suffering"? And how much does it tell us to learn—à la neo-evolutionism—that every aspect of human cognition, human emotion, human anatomy and therefore human suffering has its source in human evolution? This may be satisfactory for the nontheist, but others will still ask the question, why? Why *this* kind of cosmos? Why based on *these* principles? Why *this* type of world with *this* form of carbon-based life? We will see, especially in part III, that there are many more "whys" than can be accounted for in neo-evolutionist theory.

Are all theological and metaphysical "solutions" to the problem of evil "worthless and unnecessary"? Admittedly, they haven't taken us very far. But, then, have we derived any ultimate answers from science? This is in no way meant to denigrate scientific achievement but simply to question the tendency towards *scientism*, the unquestioning faith in science to solve every problem. Perhaps by the very nature of things all we can expect, even from science, are orientations and intimations. At the boundaries of science we come up against the inherent limitations of human understanding. Neo-evolutionism—despite its claims—does not tell us everything. At the edge of scientific enquiry we encounter the chasm between what science describes and what the mind can comprehend.

As a digression, we might ask whether this should make for abject pessimism. Do we, as the Psalmist said, "walk in a vain shadow" (Psalms 39)? Long ago, the philosopher Bertrand Russell suggested that "all the labours of the ages, all the devotion, all the inspiration, all the noonday brightness of human genius, are destined to extinction in the vast death of the solar system, and that the whole temple of Man's achievement must inevitably be buried beneath the debris of a universe in ruins" (quoted by Richardson 1966, 15–16). A scientific appreciation of the cosmos, as we shall see (part III), does not have to lead to this conclusion. At least, this does not tell us the whole story.

The neo-evolutionist argument is really another, more refined form of materialism, the view that nothing exists, or presumably has ever existed, except matter. The commonly accepted way of attacking this kind of materialism is by making counterclaims. Theists, for instance, will argue that divinity, the soul, and values have an independent existence and that matter therefore is not the only reality. C. E. M. Joad succinctly summarizes the antimaterialist viewpoint, "I hold that the universe contains at least three different orders or realms of being. There are the material constituents of which the physical world is composed; . . . there are the minds which are aware of them, and there is a third order . . . certain changeless and eternal objects (or qualities) such as truth, goodness, beauty, and maybe deity which are neither mental or material" (1932, 259–60).

However, such counterclaims are liable to be refuted by the argument that even such nonmaterial objects/qualities have a material source. Can we, for instance, deny the biochemical origins of musical ideas or of the sound waves that transport them? Yet we may still suspect—contrary to what appears to be scientific evidence—that a Beethoven symphony or an André Previn jazz improvization is more than a collection of neurons. (This is really just a restatement of the mind-body/brain problem, which is also unresolved.) The materialist maintains that to invoke a divine agency as a deus ex machina just will not do, but the materialist argument is equally unfalsifiable. The contention that nothing exists except matter becomes meaningless because an argument that purports to explain everything explains nothing. Whatever view we take, it still doesn't explain why there is—or should be—evil. If it is a choice between the ignorance of belief and the ignorance of unbelief, it seems, on the evidence such as we have, that the theists have as good a case as any.

Neither materialism nor nonmaterialism necessarily imply that nature is progressive in the sense that it is programmed to produce higher and better forms of life. Yet, as part of the highly diversified extravaganza of evolution, this is undoubtedly what has happened. Nature may not be perfective or benevolent. There may be no pre-determined goal, but the process of selection and adaptation has, in general, determined life chances in the survival stakes. Progress is very difficult to define. Progress for what and for whom? Progress in what way? Steady progress (unilinear) or staggered progress (epi-sodic)? Such qualifying questions have to be asked. Biologist George Williams is even hesitant about the idea of "cumulative progress" (1966). But despite all the doubts, the definitional niceties, and the current predilections for seeing "nature as one," we can hardly dis-pute that humans are a stage or two above flatworms.

If we move from what the nineteenth century theorist Herbert Spencer called the organic (the biological world) to the superor-ganic (the social world), the notion of progress becomes even more contestable. Has there been appreciable *moral* development? We are aware—contrary to one-time popular myth—that members of other species do attack and kill one another, but humans have added a whole new dimension to the exercise of aggression. This is intelligi-ble—though not excusable—by virtue of their history. The exigen-cies of evolution—the struggle for resources, for territory and, not least, for position and status—have all contributed to our being the way we are. Though whether it can ever be assumed—à la Freud—that we will ever outgrow those "primitive instincts" is very much open to doubt. Selection and adaptation mean different things in the social world where the process is controlled, or *can be* controlled, by conscious deliberation—something of which war is obviously the measure.

Intelligence—whatever that may mean—and what we call self-awareness has its own price. This, as we all know, has to be paid in terms of misery and suffering. In the struggle for security and well-being, we must all eventually lose. The drive for self-fulfillment and esteem are likewise elusive and ephemeral goals. Wasn't it Walt Whitman who said that man was nature's only worrier? Yet self-awareness is one of our most prized possessions. Its product is mind—matter conscious of itself.

The root of moral evil is seen by some neo-evolutionists not as something innate but as the clash between the interests of one individual and another. Are we to suppose, then, that an individual living in complete isolation is completely free of evil? He may not have any social obligations, but he may still entertain corrosive thoughts, recollections, bitterness, and hostility. Furthermore, we must ask why it is that individuals respond in the way they do when their interests are threatened. Isn't this because we all have the innate capacity, if not the proclivity, for aggression? It is hardly possible to explain human experience without making such an assumption. On the other hand, in recognizing the complex interplay of both nature and nurture in the makeup of the individual personality, neo-revolutionists are surely right in refuting the arguments of those who maintain that it is nurture that is the more dominant force. Some theorists are ideologically committed to such a view and wish to see humans as fundamentally good people who are corrupted by social factors, although it is quite untenable both historically and experientially (see Carlton 1990).

There are potentially answerable and unanswerable questions, but to ask *why* evil exists is not the same as asking *how* it came to exist. One cannot (as Anders did, 1994, 333–34) simply reformulate one in terms of the other or dismiss the seemingly unanswerable out of hand. Neither, of course, presents problems for those who find such questions meaningless. Yet there are those of us who feel compelled to ask such questions *and* do something to calm our troubled spirits, as well as satisfy our intellectual curiosity. I confess I am at the water's edge with this one, with no clear plan on how to proceed. But in the following coda (part III), I am determined to seek—although I may well not find—the faintest clue to a possible answer. That will be the just penalty for my presumption.

# Part III

## Coda

# 9

## Rationality and Belief

IN THE PHILOSOPHY OF RELIGION THERE IS RARELY, IF EVER, A CONSISTENT answer to any problem. This specially applies when discussing the *rationality* of particular beliefs. In the mundane world, rationality is inextricably related to *proof*. As far as religion is concerned, it is a question of what can and cannot be proved. And where definite proof is not available, is there even a plausible explanation?

Theistic belief entails a recognition of a supranatural or divine agency that is immanently or transcendentally related to the world order. This belief can be seen as rational if proof of such an agency exists (NB, this is not quite the same as saying that belief is rational *only if* there is proof of such existence). Here it is important to note the elementary distinction between *deductive* statements in which the premises appear to provide positive evidence for the conclusion and *inductive* statements that are made on the basis of probability only.

It is also important to make clear at the outset of our discussion that if a proof is to be seen as *valid*, the premises must be related logically to the conclusion (though it should be borne in mind that a conclusion can be true even though the construction of the argument is invalid—a point that is particularly pertinent to arguments about religion). Furthermore, an argument should be *sound*. A person may have a rational belief that the proof is sound, even though this does not guarantee that the ultimate conclusion *is* rational. In other words, true premises must result in a true conclusion, but *belief* in the validity of the premises does not have to determine a correct conclusion. It almost goes without saying that in all arguments one must distinguish between statements of fact and statements of value which are often opinions propounded as if they were facts. Again, not at all uncommon in discussions about religion.

While we are making distinctions, perhaps we should remind ourselves that we are primarily concerned here with the problem *of* evil and not the critical but more mundane problem *with* evil. The former raises technical philosophical questions, while the latter pertains to more everyday issues of a personal and social nature. Evil has been of general concern to societies since time immemorial, and so much religious practice has been devoted to the task of either warding off evil (as pain, misfortune, etc.) or, complementarily, securing benefits from the gods. As we have seen, rituals such as sacrifices, benefactions, oblations, and so forth have not been merely expressions of gratitude to the spirits but also attempts to elicit their favors. We can take one simple—and to modern minds, simplistic— example. At the great purification feast in Inca Peru, the people made cakes of maize flour and children's blood and rubbed themselves with the mixture in an attempt to counter various diseases. Four royal Inca acting as messengers and representing the Sun God (Inti) commanded the diseases to depart, whereupon the people rejoiced and praised the "messengers" who had exorcised the spirits of evil (Katz 2000, 203). It appears baffling to us how people could believe in such rituals that were patently quite ineffective and which presumably had to be repeated over and over again. As polytheists, they appear not to have had a problem *of* evil because of the benevolent Sun God (who shared the pantheon with others and was therefore not alone in his dealings with the people), although even he could be somewhat arbitrary from time to time—hence the rescue services of the Rain God.

A variant can be found in early sixth century BC classical society, where the Athenian lawgiver Solon saw the city being progressively corroded by greed, strife, and the unreasonable demands of its citizens and warned that if this continued Zeus would bring down destruction. He, like Plato many years later, had a sense of cosmic justice that attended even the best of human endeavors. The view was that there was an indissoluble link between the human and divinely controlled worlds, where the gods—for good or ill—always had the initiative (Castleden 1998, 171).

The irrationality of these and other similar attitudes and procedures in prescientific society is mirrored in some ways in our own society. Superstition is not dead. Amulets and charms are still popular and are sometimes adopted by those with orthodox religious beliefs—hardly a pragmatic approach. There is no clear evidence for their efficacy, and it must be presumed that people are intent on hedging their bets and taking out a little extra-celestial insurance.

Whatever means people employ to contact or supplicate otherworldly powers, even if it is to no apparent effect, the belief (or hope) persists that such forces exist and that whether they are demons or divinities, it pays to humor and appease them. In practice, it appears to make little difference whether we are dealing with High Religions or primitive tribal cults. The concerns are much the same. People desperately want to believe that evil can be averted and that life can be made more predictable and secure. Even in modern secular society, there is evidence that there is still a vestigial suspicion that there may be something beyond the manifest and mundane world. But religion here is often tainted by the prevailing hedonism. Note those forms of evangelism in the West which are predicated upon that U.S. import, the "Gospel of Prosperity," where to be a believer is to get rich, and be happy.

The very fact that none of these strategies can be shown unambiguously to bring results in terms of either health or happiness, regardless of what is claimed, generates the nature of our problem. The obvious conclusion then is that either: (a) our faith is ill-founded, that our ideas about divinity and the existence of the supramundane world are mistaken or in some way ill-conceived (e.g., are the gods indifferent?) or (b) our faith is inadequate, that we are unworthy creatures and cannot therefore expect or merit the benefits we crave.

In tackling the first of these possibilities, we must look briefly at the age-old question of proof of the existence of god(s). The standard "proofs" have long been called into question, most notably by Kant, but it should be recognized that one, the *argument from design*, which we will consider in due course, has probably more cogency than the others.

The *ontological proof* hinges on the assumption that God must exist because we cannot conceive of a being who is greater than God. Or to put it another way, is the nonexistence of God conceivable? That which can be conceived not to exist is ipso facto not God. Yet it must be asked if existence is a predicate. This argument has the customary annoying circularity and can never be conclusive. But can it even be persuasive?

Kant himself favored the *moral proof.* Here the argument is that moral obligation would carry no conviction (thus moral life would make no sense) if there were no God. In Kant's formulation, there is a universal moral law for everyone, primitive and sophisticate alike. All have an abiding sense of "ought" and "ought not." For different people—and certainly for different cultures—this may be applied in different ways, but everyone has a compelling sense of obligation about *something*. It is a universal moral imperative. Proponents of the moral-proof position insist that if we are serious about moral issues this argument must have some resonance. But a really persuasive argument contains a proof of its own premises. How can it be shown that morality requires a deity as its ultimate validation? And this entirely discounts the *specific* nature of moral rules themselves and their actual application.

The complementary arguments from design have a lot more going for them. The *cosmological proof* is argued from initial causes. Its basic premise is that it is not possible to get something from nothing, something still being debated by cosmologists who, understandably, are not prepared to hazard views about what came before the beginning or what "caused" the beginning (indeed, some would regard the question as meaningless). We live in a contingent world, and, so it is argued, this implies a divine agency. This view is supported by a qualified *teleological* argument which not only maintains that design requires a designer but also that the design itself is undeniably purposive. From our foregoing discussion (part I), we can see that this approach is fraught with problems (a position most famously associated with David Hume). Yet, having said this, the created world does exhibit all sorts of interesting features that may not be simply ascribed to pure chance.

The idea of *experiential* proof begs just too many questions. Whose experience are we talking about? And how does the experience of A conform to or differ from that of the experience of B? To what extent are experiences influenced or determined by the nature of the religious traditions in question? What are the patterns of expectation—does the expected become the experienced? Furthermore, if we concede that someone has had a genuinely unusual experience, how is this to be interpreted? (note, particularly the experience of "speaking in tongues" found among a number of believers and specifically cultivated among certain religious communities, e.g., Pentecostals. Is it a "holy language" or simply gibberish? And is there here a confusion between glossolalia and xenolalia, i.e., miraculously speaking in a known but unlearned foreign language?) The problems with the experiential approach are obvious. "Proofs" that are based on instinct or intuition, however interpreted, can never be more than well-meaning assertions, as far as other people are concerned. They belong to the realms of mysticism rather than serious philosophical debate.

There are those who, in their search for empirical criteria for theism, resort to *consequential proofs*. Their argument is that the better (nobler? more moral?) the belief system, the more worthy will be the consequences. (This reminds me of the standard refutations of those critics who allege that the fervor and excitement of an evangelistic meeting is no different from that of a Nuremberg rally or even a pop concert. That may well be the case, but presumably the *consequences* will be different.) Again, the argument has a certain cogency but can never be conclusive because there are so many exceptions to the rule. Another form of the consequences argument relates to the derivation of higher human values, "where do all the good impulses in human nature come from? Whence all the readiness to find and serve the truth, to banish ignorance and superstition, to seek a just and equal social order, to destroy the ugly and create the beautiful . . . ? Are they simply the products of merely human longing and nothing more? And why are they frustrated at every turn, so that the human nature which conceives and desires [them] is so impotent to bring them to fulfilment?" (Richardson 1966, 117). Here a theologian is quite clearly advancing the thesis that virtue is god-given.

It is interesting how this approach to theism differs from that of Kirkegaard, who held that any kind of rational proof actually militated against theism. Instead he insisted that subjectivism was paramount, and opted—in his typically contrary way—for "objective uncertainty" because he believed that the virtues of theism would be destroyed by any evidence in its favor.

Even more adventurous are those who seek *experimental proofs* in terms of the paranormal. Indeed, parapsychology has, for some, become either a way of substantiating theism, or, for others, an alternative to religion (Gregory 1981). In a fairly recent study among students in Higher Education (Carlton 2000), it was found that respondents generally made no very clear distinction between "religious experiences" and what they felt to be paranormal (unusual?) experiences. Some rather more conservative students, on the other hand, actually suggested that paranormal carried an attribution of evil—a sort of dabbling with demonic forces that are best left undisturbed. Others, however, felt that parapsychological investigation might provide some evidential support for religious ideas and perhaps even confirm the existence of an other-worldly dimension. For the more theistically inclined, there was an understandable tendency to want to harmonize experiences, and it was not always recognized that if one develops a guiding fiction for reconciling the intellectually discordant and the emotionally unusual, once formed this may be very resistant to change. Nevertheless, it was thought by many that religion can be distinguished by its moral force and by its capacity for personality modification.

It would appear, therefore, that any genuine evidence is welcome. There are surely few people who would not like to know, to understand, simply to discern some meaning in the order of things. And it is the problem of theodicy—however it is formulated—that is the great stumbling block. But is this because our conception of divinity is misconceived? Hence the various forms of dualism that, by definition, require an evil as well as a good agency.

The dualistic system par excellence is Zoroastrianism, which arose in Iran and can be approximately dated to the sixth century BC, thus preceding its near contemporaries, Buddhism, Taoism, and Confucianism. Zoroaster or Zarathushtra, its legendary founder, is said to have been so perplexed about the problems of good and evil, suffering and death that he went into isolation and there spent agonizing months in prayer and meditation. He eventually came away none the wiser and was about to abandon his quest when he suddenly had what he felt to be a flash of enlightenment. If God is good, he cannot create evil, and evil cannot create good. There are thus *two* forces contending for the human soul, Ahura Mazda, the good god of light and purity, and Ahriman, the force of darkness and death. This cosmic struggle would ultimately result in the triumph of good. But in the meantime this necessitated human cooperation, for evil would only finally be banished on the Day of Judgement.

Zoroastrianism is now something of a religion in exile. Today it has relatively few adherents, but just a glance at its main tenets shows that its influence on some other religious systems has been significant. Its dualist premises are more than implicit in the teachings of the Early Church (the God versus Satan issue) but were modified by the Medieval Church, which condemned the so-called Manichean heresy. It is evident too in Judaism and in Islam, where Allah is said to be the absolute judge of all things and the One of whom no evil can be predicated. But orthodox Islam, while stressing Allah's compassion, tends to evade the onus of actually attributing evil—or what we class as evil—to his agency.

Thus we are left in all the monotheistic religions with an explicit or implicit malevolent force—a force that may be amorphous or personified, but potent and pervasive nevertheless. Belief in such an agency is one way in which those who hold that creation is purposive can avoid the conclusion that divinity is capricious. In Judaism, we can see how such thinking develops and is modified. To take one simple example, in the Old Testament (2 Sam. 24:1) we are told that Yahweh caused the king, David, to commit the sin of "numbering the people" (why such a census should be considered wrong is not made at all clear). But much later (1 Chron. 21) it is Satan who is said to provoke David to commit a sinful act, because by this time Yahweh is seen as altogether righteous and therefore incapable of such inconsistent behavior. Evil is considered contrary to his nature, so it has to be attributed to another agency.

The concept of Satan (the "adversary") is not well developed in the Old Testament and is here introduced as a "solution" to a specific philosophical problem. This is followed through by some New Testament writers. "God is Light, and in him is no darkness at all" (1 John 1:5), and "Let no one say when he is tried, 'My temptation is from God'; for God is incapable of being tempted to do evil, and He Himself tempts no one" (James 1:13). But neither offers any further solution to the problem except to stress that humans are responsible for every kind of moral evil. Unsatisfactory as this may be, it is preferable to certain Eastern faiths such as Hinduism, in which evil, like life itself, is little more than an illusion.

So can we avoid dualism? From the earliest times it has obviously been seen as the most "rational" form of explanation. As long ago as the Egyptian Old Kingdom (circa 2600–2150 BC), we find references to a conflict between the benevolent agency Osiris (possibly an early ruler who was later deified) and his evil brother Seth (again, possibly an early tribal leader representing the arid desert who was also later deified). The myth of Osiris; his sister-wife, Isis; and their successor offspring, Horus, underwent numerous changes over time. It was at the heart of Egyptian popular religion, which existed in tandem with the royal/aristocratic solar cult that effectively supported and endorsed the institution of kingship. But even this myth involved its own form of dualism. The *Pyramid Texts* tell how at death the king was believed to "ascend to the sky among the imperishable stars" and there join his father Amon-Re (the Sun), where he would journey across the heavens in the "ship of millions of years" (Kamil 1996, 88). But this was not all. The journey was not uneventful, for every night, the divine company had to overcome the god of darkness, the monster Apophis (night), in order to reemerge triumphant at dawn on the eastern horizon. Only in this way was Ma'at, the harmonius balance of the cosmos, precariously maintained.

A similar scenario with clear dualistic features can be seen in other ancient religious systems. As with the later Higher Religions, dualism or a polytheistic variant seems to be the only way of coming to terms with the antinomies of human experience. And in such systems, the evil agency is always represented as a pervasive, though ultimately defeated, potent force.

It almost goes without saying that the myths of earlier peoples are replete with stories of demons and sundry evil creatures who plague their impotent victims. And their doings, albeit often in sanitized forms, have become incorporated in religious systems that are still very much with us. One of the best examples can be found in the totally bizarre antics of Hindu deities such as those of the Nagas, semi-divine beings who were paradoxically both beneficent and vengeful—a belief still found vestigially in Bangladesh. Little is known of the pre-Indo-Aryan people whose centers in the Indus Valley (before circa 1500 BC) at Mohenjo-Daro and Harappa have yet to be thoroughly investigated. Their syllabic script has yet to be deciphered (seemingly a fairly hopeless task unless a bilingual, possibly Chaldean, text is discovered), but it is believed that we are dealing with a characteristic, priest-dominated society. The religious system changed, so it is believed, with the coming of the Aryans, possibly from Iran or the Caucasus. They were reputedly a warrior people who introduced "sky-gods" into the Pantheon. With the coming of Indra (as recounted in the sacred Vedas), also came caste distinctions, with the light-skinned Aryan invaders constituting a military-priestly elite.

The demonic agencies within Hindu mythology may stem from pre-Aryan society. The asuras, rakshakas, and pisakas (vampires), as they were popularly known, were part of common folklore. But the most significant evil deities were to be found among the Hindu high gods, such as the terrible Kali, who is usually depicted as a dark-skinned woman (a hint of the pre-Aryan indigenes), sword in hand and engorged with blood, wearing a necklace of human skulls. Ravanna, the chief of the rakshakas, is portrayed as a huge man who has ten heads and twenty arms that immediately grow again whenever they are cut off—all possibly symbolic of the ostensibly unconquerable nature of evil.

Even in the avowedly non-theistic received wisdom of Buddhism we find the Buddha (Gotama) himself being tempted by Mara, the "Prince of Darkness" who has assumed visible form. Gotama is offered the chance to be an earthly ruler, if only he will give up his quest for enlightenment. When spurned, Mara threatens to pursue his quarry and do his best to deter him from his sacred mission. Then in a second, and critical, series of temptations, we are told that the god of evil "mobilized all his friends throughout the universe [including] demons of every conceivable shape, all of equal horror, threatening and cajoling . . . [plus] a host of aerial temptresses hoping to arouse his sensuality" (Tomlin 1986, 164). Needless to say, the young Gotama resisted all attempts to divert him from his dedicated task, thus demonstrating the real yet limited power of the evil forces.

There are echoes here of monsters of all kinds, from gorgons to furies whose delight it is to harass and often destroy their human playthings. Stories of a similar kind, often fantastical in the extreme, can apparently be found in all cultures, but all obviously evince the same concern—how to account for misfortune, suffering, and death, particularly when it appears to be unfortuitous and undeserved.

Western theologians are reluctant to entertain the idea of dualism. As monotheists, along with Jews and Muslims, they find it difficult to think in terms of two contending deities. Yet dualists are not arguing for two "self-created" gods, as some monotheists seem to suppose. Rather their view is of a supreme deity and a lesser divinity who has a temporary ascendency for reasons which, to humans, are quite inexplicable. So the God-versus-Satan conception would fit neatly into such a scenario. Evil therefore has a personalized or unknown cause. As Plato put it, "few are the goods of human life, and many are the evils, and the good alone is to be attributed to God; of the evils the causes are to be sought elsewhere . . ." (quoted by Robinson 1946, 32).

Similar views have been echoed in more recent times by would-be theists. H. G. Wells, for instance, toyed quite seriously for a while with a form of dualism in which the good god is the lesser deity who will ultimately triumph with the help of humanity. In a greatly modified form, dualist ideas were part of philosopher C. E. M. Joad's theism. The late Professor C. S. Lewis, a specialist in English literature who also established a considerable reputation as a writer of children's books and as a popular apologist for theism, makes a case for a demonic agency, indeed, very amusingly, in his perceptive *Screwtape Letters*. His views on suffering (*The Problem of Pain*), however, seem to me to be somewhat flawed. He argues that if one accepts the providence of God, one must therefore accept that if God could have created a better world he would have done so (note Albert Einstein's similar, but cosmological, dilemma). Therefore, evil must be seen as the inevitable consequence of the decision that it is better for human beings to be free personalities rather than machines—a plausible argument which, as we have already seen, begs innumerable questions, not least those concerning natural (or cosmic) evil. As God's omnipotence does not include the power to do that which is intrinsically impossible or ridiculous, it has to be that it must be equally impossible to create a world of free personalities in which there is no pain or evil.

C. S. Lewis appears to have no problem with the idea of a personal devil and goes so far as to suggest that he may have been at work in the universe before humans came on the scene. He speculates that the devil's task, or intention, was the corruption of the created order, and this spoiling activity has resulted in the suffering we see at every level in the world of nature. So carnivores were presumably once law-abiding herbivores, but what of the multiplicity of parasites, viruses, bacteria, and the like? Was their nature transformed by this same evil agency? And if we can accept, just for the sake of argument, that this is what actually took place, why was it allowed to happen? Can this be squared with the idea of a benevolent deity?

Even more uncertain are C. S. Lewis's rather casuistical contentions about pain itself. He maintains that the problem of pain is not made more grave by the multiplication of the instances of pain. Or to look at it another way, when we have found the maximum amount of pain that any person can suffer, we have found the greatest amount of pain there is. The addition of countless other sufferers does not increase this pain. (It is a little like the argument that if $x$ equals infinity, then $x$ multiplied by infinity also equals $x$). It is an ingenious argument but only *theoretically* convincing.

C. S. Lewis, who was once an atheist but who became convinced of the rationality of theism, had few doubts about the nature of evil. He endorsed the church's teaching on the fundamental theological issues, so it might be as well to see how its views on personalized evil derive. Before the Exile (the deportation of part of the population of Judah to Babylon in 586 BC), the Old Testament records nothing of the Devil or Satan, unless we interpret the "serpent" in the Garden of Eden story as symbolizing the spirit of evil. It may then be reasonable to assume that much of the demonology and angelology found later in Judaism and in the church were importations from Mesopotamia. They were certainly not part of the teaching of the great eighth-century prophets. The Book of Job—admittedly difficult to date, but which in its final drama-like form is probably post-Exilic—introduces us to Satan, the "accuser." In the Prologue, he is depicted as a heavenly being, one of the "sons of God" who acts as a kind of public prosecutor. Job, he argues, though ostensibly a good man, is really suspect because he behaves as he does because it pays him to do so. His "goodness" is simply a matter of self-interest. If put to the test, one would soon see the kind of man he really was. Even so, it is very doubtful whether one could construct a theory of evil or of a personalized evil agency on the basis of this one book.

There are references to the devil in some of the books of the Apocrypha and in some other noncanonical treatises that have not found a wide acceptance. It was in the period between the Testaments that the rival schools of the Pharisees and the Sadducees arose, the one endorsing the existence of angels and demons that the other denied. Before long, the former traditions had given rise to the conception of a complex hierarchy of good and evil spirits which was even further elaborated in the Medieval Church.

The New Testament is replete with references to a personalized evil agency (Satan, diabolos, daimon, etc.), and we cannot doubt that regardless of the reinterpretations of liberal theologians, these beliefs were sincerely held in the Primitive Church. Should they therefore be discarded along with erroneous cosmological ideas and the simple views of geography, physiology, and the like that are tacitly assumed in these early writings? Or must we give these seemingly naive ideas more credence?

The key issue for believers centers on the authority of the scriptures. Are they a vehicle of revelation or aren't they? Are believers—is posterity—lumbered with a collection of oudated superstitions, or are there here certain truths that are not only valuable but also eternal? Some exegetes see all references to the devil as necessarily metaphorical—a concession to current, popular thought. But although some references may be seen in these terms, others such as the Temptation (recorded in the three synoptic Gospels) cannot easily be interpreted in this way. And then we have such cryptic allusions to Satan "falling as lightening from heaven" (Luke 10:18). What are we to make of such sayings?

It cannot be denied that for the early community of believers such an evil force was an ever-present reality. The Book of Acts makes this quite clear, as do many of the Epistles. In these, and preeminently in the Book of Revelation, the devil/Satan is seen variously as an "adversary," as a "deceiver," and as "Prince of This World," the controller of the realm outside the church. Though it needs to be asked to what extent this hypothesized evil power was in some way associated with the pervasive, repressive power of Rome which was in the process of persecuting the early Christians. Or can these be effectively distinguished? Can there possibly be entities/spiritual influences which lie outside the human domain and were once recognized by earlier peoples as demons, malevolent spirits, and the like?

This presents us with a fanciful, yet possible, science-fiction scenario. Many cultures trace their gods to some disruption in the cosmic realm. "The war in heaven" scenario is common, not least in certain Jewish apocalyptic books and in Greek mythology where Kronos is attacked by his own offspring. The rebellion that is alluded to in Christian mythology is similar, except that here it is the unjustified act of a once-favored subordinate deity. Was there a "fall" of some kind beyond the human sphere? Possibly an intragalactic conflict that has had disastrous repercussions for our particular world? The whole thing smacks of *Star Wars* but does go some way towards a possible explanation. After all, for monotheists, if God did not create evil, then evil must represent the primal rebellion of some created will. But if such an explanation *is* accepted, it merely puts back the problem one stage. Why was such a rebellion not crushed? Why was the evil force allowed to continue? Is it too powerful? If so, we are back with a form of dualism.

A further variant of the dualist position has been adopted by a number of theorists, not least the late C. E. M. Joad who contends that there is here a real problem that must be faced. "It is not so much a case of saying we do not understand; the difficulty is greater than that. It is a case rather of something we cannot understand because it is not understandable. [Yet although] there may be a mystery at the heart of things . . . the mystery should not be such as to outrage our reason" (1942, 42–43). Joad maintained that a benevolent deity did not create evil; neither is evil entirely the result of human free will. He accepts that there may be discarnate spirits and that there may have been some primary celestial conflict that ultimately impinged on the human realm. But he argues that the forces unleashed are *not* self-created and being therefore not self-existent their power, though considerable, is limited.

Thus far, Joad has endorsed the orthodox dualist position. But here he parts company with normal dualism and proposes a somewhat more refined "solution." He is joined by some modern theologians in insisting that, for reasons so far unexplained, God is unable (not unwilling) to deal with these malevolent powers. This impotent deity "answer" is certainly kinder to God because it implies that God would really like to help if he could. But it still doesn't really solve the problem, unless we assume that these recalcitrant spirits (or spirit) are, like humans, possessed of independent capacities which the deity cannot overrule. Yet even this presents difficulties. Because if monotheistic religion is saying anything, it is saying that ultimately good *will* triumph. But *when*? And why the seemingly inordinate delay?

This was the concern of the Early Church. The terrible sacrifices made by persecuted believers were predicated on the imminent "end of the age." The apostle Paul wrote of the entire creation agonizing in anticipation of its redemption. The "parousia" was to be the culmination of all that believers had hoped and worked for, but Paul had to warn them against precipitate action (well-documented among millennialist groups) or early disappointment.

The idea of a deity who, though benevolent, is nevertheless impotent is a theme famously elaborated by Dietrich Bonhoeffer, who was executed by the Nazis shortly before the end of the Second World War. In *The Courage to Be* he not only writes of the "powerlessness of God" and of the "suffering of God" who "conquers . . . the world by his weakness," he also argues that we should learn to live in the world without using God as a working hypothesis (quoted by Robinson 1963, 39). In effect, Bonhoeffer is saying that we must abandon conventional theology and that we can avoid disappointment about the parousia or anything else if we "mature" and recognize, as Julien Huxley once insisted, that the God hypothesis is no longer of any pragmatic value for the interpretation or comprehension of nature. He concedes that conventional religion will still be found necessary to cope with the "so-called ultimate questions—death, guilt—on which only 'God' can furnish an answer. . . . But what if one day they no longer exist as such, if they too can be answered without 'God'?" (Robinson 1963, 37).

It has to be admitted that in science, politics, and ethics (and, some might cynically argue, even in religion) God is not required, or possibly expected, to guarantee anything, to solve anything, or even to intervene in human affairs. Thus evil—insofar as it is recognized at all—is not a religious issue because there is no longer any recognition of a cosmic problem, and therefore no anticipation of a cosmic solution. The traditional Christian answer that evil has already been effectively defeated by the Crucifixion and ultimately the

Resurrection is not seen as tenable, nor is its potential acknowledged. Yet even these purported "great acts" have been called into question by liberal thinkers and are said to be virtually incomprehensible to "a world come of age." Purely naturalist as well as supernaturalist interpretations are repudiated: the naturalist because it reduces the entire religious philosophy to meaninglessness and the supernaturalist because it endorses claims that are quite implausible—claims, indeed, that can make vestigial sense only if the supporting documentary evidence is suitably demythologized.

Here again we are back with the problem of evil. The doctrine—or *one* doctrine—of the Atonement may be a highly mythological representation of a dubious transaction between God and the devil, whereby a ransom is paid to release the world from the burden of sin. That the Early Church interpreted the Crucifixion in this way probably says more about the legacy of Judaism and theories of pagan sacrificial rituals than anything else. The deus-ex-machina intervention seems to be straight out of Greek tragedy. Can evil be bought off in this way? Is this a once-and-for-all act that has monumental cosmic implications, as some believers claim? Or does it symbolize rather something more mundane yet very profound—a conjunction of forces, political expediency, institutionalized religion, entrenched attitudes, and a seemingly infinite capacity of the public to be manipulated? Did evil conspire with gross human stupidity in the murder of innocence?

We can either confront evil in whatever form it takes, or we can assume a totally fatalistic attitude and resign ourselves to its presence. On the other hand, with the neo-evolutionists we may deny its objective reality and content ourselves with the thought that what is termed evil is simply part of the perplexing vagaries of the everyday world. But the theist cannot wholly adopt any one of these theoretical positions unreservedly. Theists confront the *fact* of evil, even though they feel that their capacity to combat it may be severely limited. They may do their best to live up to the light they have—yet frequently fail. They may make some modest contribution to making the world a better place—but progress in this task, as we know too well, is pathetically slow. Regardless of the ideologies, religious or political, which proclaim otherwise, neither we nor the world are perfectible.

What is critical for the theist is that the *problem* of evil (which really means the problem of theodicy) does not undermine his belief in the plan and purpose of a benevolent deity. This is his ultimate concern, his "sacred canopy." Without faith his life is devoid of direction and meaning. Yet perhaps there are ways in which science may come to theism's aid by suggesting not so much solutions as indicating certain confirmatory possibilities. After all, if one can ask the questions, there *has* to be an answer.

# 10

## Theism and Science

Why is there something rather than nothing? Perhaps the greatest puzzle about the cosmos is that it exists at all. Wasn't it Einstein who once remarked that the most beautiful experience is that "feeling of the mysterious"?

Is the cosmos simply the result of a quantum fluctuation—a primordial "incident" with no apparent cause? If so, it can therefore have no obvious purpose or be imbued with implicit moral dimensions. Thus good and evil can be seen as mere humanly imposed qualities—values that have a convenient social utility. Adversity, which is understandably regarded as a curse, then becomes an essential ingredient in the struggle for survival. Evil, or what has come to be seen as evil, is then part of a blind developmental process which eliminates the unfit and facilitates progress by a series of random mutations. Ergo, do we agree with the optimists who say that this is the best of all possible worlds, or with the pessimists who cynically argue that they may well be right?

This is the essence of the evolutionary thesis. But is it really persuasive? Do *all* these things that we have come to regard as evil, both natural and moral, actually conduce to anything that we can reasonably construe as progress? The crunch question is, do we live in a rationally conceived, or a randomly indeterminate, universe? Is there any sense in which the universe is "intelligent," perhaps not for human advantage but for some purpose that is beyond our comprehension?

We may as well admit from the outset that we are never going to find a final or definitive answer to the problem of theodicy. The best we can do is to suggest arguments that support, however tentatively, the view that despite all indications to the contrary, life may be the creation of a benevolent, or at least purposive, deity.

One of the great misunderstandings of our time is that the incredible progress in scientific achievement and the consequent increase in the prestige of the natural sciences has led to a serious undermining of theism. Belief in God is uncertain. The *belief itself* can be demonstrated, but the existence of supranatural entities cannot possibly be verified by the scientific method. But then neither can a great many other things in life. If A says to B "I love you," by what criteria can such a statement be proved? It is certainly not open to falsification—though an unfalsifiable statement is not necessarily an untrue statement.

With subsequent doubt has gone a denial of divine design and the notion of a purposive universe. It is still commonly held that theism is only entertained because it is a comforting thought to believe in a God who is concerned for his creatures. Such ideas are said to be, as Marx argued, mere projections of the human psyche, or, as Freud similarly argued, consolatory illusions that really belong to an earlier stage in the evolutionary process. Yet it should be fairly obvious that the function of religion, both at the social and individual level, extends beyond that of mere amorphous wish fulfillment. (Anyhow, is wish fulfillment necessarily bad? A wish does not necessarily invalidate the reality or legitimacy of that which is wished for.) It hardly needs to be stressed that the existence of false beliefs does not invalidate the fact of an underlying true belief.

Doubts are also often expressed about "revealed religion," often by believers themselves. They dispute the value of historical/documentary evidence that seems to support the claims of devotees, and argue instead for convictions based on subjective awareness. But then we all know just how unreliable intuitive impressions can be. Where logical or demonstrative proof is lacking, it is tempting, though ultimately unconvincing, to fall back on experiential assertions that constitute a kind of reality to the individuals concerned.

Equally uncertain is the claim, à la Kant, that a divine agency is necessary to authorize or validate ethical values. Yet it is also unwise to regard all such values as mere products of social necessity. Values are surely not simply formulated solely on the basis of social utility? If we adopt this kind of ethical relativism, we are ultimately enmeshed in an infinite regression that can have no satisfactory resolution.

There are no conclusive evidential "proofs" for theism, but there are those "transcendental signals" to which we have already alluded. Primarily we are concerned here with arguments from design and the whole idea of a purposive creation. We can, I feel, treat with reserve Kant's refutation of the so-called "cosmological proof," simply on the basis that there can be no causal connection between God, who is, by definition, outside nature and nature itself. It would seem that there is nothing contrary to scientific reasoning in positing a causal relationship between spirit and matter, i.e., between deity and the physical universe. Fundamentally, we are faced with the alternative either of a creation that has emerged by sheer chance or of a perplexing yet ordered universe. Either the cosmos is fortuitous and purposeless, or it exists for some intelligent, if inscrutable, reason. If we accept the argument from design, we then have to decide whether we are dealing with a providential principle or/and a maleficent principle and, if they exist, just how these powers are to be assessed.

By the end of the nineteenth century, it was claimed that the basic outline of the natural world was all but complete. Nature's grand plan was now well understood, and all that was now required was to fill in the details. Indeed, when the noted physicist Max Planck, then a young scholar, was at the point of considering a career in physics research, he was discouraged by his professor, who assured him that the prospect of further significant developments was unlikely. Fortunately, he ignored the advice to seek fame elsewhere.

We now know, of course, that there were, and certainly still are, many more scientific worlds to conquer. Most fundamental of all, perhaps, is an understanding of life itself. The mechanistic manifestos of earlier theorists have proved to be grossly misleading. So, likewise, have attempts to reproduce life synthetically under laboratory conditions. No one has yet succeeded in creating a modest bacterium. Indeed, the structure and reproductive capacity of a single cell is of such amazing complexity that science doesn't really know where to begin. The components have long been identified, but what are they *really*? What makes them animate? What *is* a ribosome or a protein or an enzyme? Reduced to essentials, they are inanimate matter, but together, in some very special and still largely inexplicable way, they "become" life. Perhaps we should abandon the mechanistic/reductionist approach. As one microbiologist puts it, "We cannot hope to understand life by dissecting it. . . . [We cannot reduce life] to a collection of parts" (McFadden 2000, 12). The argument here is that taken in isolation none of the key properties of life is sufficient to define the phenomenon in question.

Furthermore, we cannot account for the apparent spontaneous generation of life. Did it arise from some fortuitous combination of circumstances some four billion years ago? And is life, in some form or another, a unique phenomenon? Is there something in the panspermia thesis which suggests that either by accident or design the earth was seeded with life spores from outer space and slowly flourished in what proved to be a conducive environment? In addition, we have the further question of why life took the forms that it did. Selection, adaptation, and the general question of survival do not adequately account for the wide variety of known species. How also can we account for the fact that living creatures have been able to direct their own actions? In higher animals such as ourselves the ability to *will* our actions seems to be in conflict with the idea (dogma?) of evolutionary determinism.

To cite the evolutionary process is to leave a lot of unanswered questions. We know that on our own planet life is carbon-based, yet there appears to be no known predetermined or common metabolic chemistry that must drive all living cells. Is life simply (if that is the term) a complex chemical reaction? If it is, then we must explain how a wide variety of chemical processes generates the same phenomenon. Or could it be that there is some essential, and so far inexplicable, quality to life that science has yet to discover?

The evolutionary process has involved not only large as well as small "leaps," it has also involved inexplicable mutations. For example, the development of DNA as a gene component is critically dependent on proteins. But all known modern proteins fall into about a thousand different "families." Yet why this should be so and how exactly these have evolved from some early antecedent family is still something of a mystery. And precisely how such complex structures such as the eye and the ear, not to mention the brain, are to be explained in biochemical terms, is still as elusive as ever. It hardly seems possible, not to say plausible, to explain them in terms of random mutations. Each small step in the evolutionary sequence, despite certain inevitable dead-ends, must represent some tiny improvement on its predecessor. According to one expert, "somehow we must account for the spontaneous emergence of a cell with enzymes, ribosomes, RNA and DNA with all the 500 or so genes of the photo-cell" (McFadden 2000, 84). What we must ask is how an organism with five hundred genes each made up of about a thousand DNA bases can have arisen entirely by chance. The late Professor Hoyle likened the chances to a tornado sweeping through a junkyard and assembling a Boeing 747.

How then do we get from the hypothesized primeval soup to the first simple cells? Given that the constituents of cells are not in themselves self-replicating, how is order generated from apparent disorder? In short, how does the animate derive from the inanimate? How can we get life from non-life?

The current Human Genome Project is at least decoding the hitherto unknown genetic "book of man." The huge DNA molecule (about one meter long) is coiled within every human cell containing twenty-three pairs of chromosomes, which carry the all-important genes that dictate the behavior of the cell. Each chromsone consists of four protein compounds that appear in a myriad of different orders. To unravel these has been a colossal task, given that there are something in the order of three billion "bases" in the twenty-three chromosomes. Such is the complexity of life.

Can life therefore be a freak accident of chemistry? Or are the properties such that life is not so much inevitable as actually *intended*? Perhaps life is not a chance happening or a lucky coincidence but the outcome of some mysterious design—Hence what is known as the anthropic principle. Such ideas do not entirely accord with the received wisdom of science. The gulf in understanding "... is a major conceptual lacuna," according to Professor Paul Davies, who is quick to assure us that he is not suggesting that life's origin was a supernatural event, only that we are "missing something very fundamental ... something with profound philosophical ramifications" (1998, xvi–xvii). Indeed, this is something about which investigators privately admit they are completely baffled.

The anthropic principle has been invoked to account for the many peculiar factors that seem to be uniquely conducive to the development of life—particularly intelligent life. Even quite a small change in these biochemical constants would mean that life—certainly life as we know it—could not exist. Why these constants possess the qualities they do is, at present, outside the scope of science. It is therefore tempting to speculate that they are as they are in order to facilitate life. The chance that they are merely fortuitous coincidences is quite beyond even the lottery pundits. Without this particular combination of factors, the emergence of life would be an extraordinarily improbable occurrence. Nobel Prize-winner Francis Crick has said that the origin of life is "almost like a miracle," so many are the conditions that must be satisfied (1981, 88). Indeed, the chance of this occurrence is so remote that some theorists are prepared to hypothesize that life as we know it has to be entirely unique. Jacques Monod has written of humanity being alone in the unfeeling immensity of the universe (1972, 167).

Not every theorist accepts, or wants to accept, the logic of the anthropic argument. But even if it can be shown that life on Earth is not a singular event, it still does not undermine the general argument about the emergence (dare one say "creation"?) of life itself. And if there is something to the anthropic principle, does it not indicate a purposeful universe, despite all the obvious anomalies?

The anthropic argument has been neatly summed up by Freeman Dyson, who writes that on studying the details of its architecture "the universe in some sense must have known we were coming" (1979, 250). Another Nobel Prize–winner, Professor de Duve, holds that life is inevitable given the right conditions. But this kind of deterministic argument gets us no further; it inevitably begs the question of just how one obtains the right conditions. Biochemistry indicates that they are not that easy to come by. If life did originate elsewhere in the cosmos, the problem has not substantially changed. It has merely put the problem of biogenesis back a stage. The question is one of how life began, whether here or elsewhere. It is not simply a matter of preferential chemical affinities. That seems more of a description than an explanation.

Perhaps Paul Davies has a point when he says that molecular biologists will look in vain for conventional physics and chemistry to explain life; this, he says, is to confuse the medium with the message. "The secret of life lies not in its chemical basis, but in the logical and informational rules it exploits. Life succeeds precisely because it *evades* chemical imperatives" (1998, 212). Even more important (and certainly, for the theist, more exciting) is the question of whether mind is somehow written into the laws of nature. It is surely significant that humans, as products of those laws, should have the capacity to understand the very laws that have given rise to that understanding in the first place. We are back with mind as matter conscious of itself.

The anthropic principle is also related to the hypothesized age of the universe. According to current cosmological theory, it takes about ten billion years of stellar evolution for generations of stars to synthesize significant quantities of heavy elements such as carbon from the primordial gases helium and hydrogen. Ergo, we could not inhabit a universe younger than ten billion years. The universe has to be large because it has to be old (i.e., old enough to allow carbon-based life to evolve). Such theorizing is the basis of what is termed the "weak anthropic principle," which is regarded as reasonably uncontroversial. What is thought to be far more contentious is the "strong anthropic principle," which maintains that the fundamental laws of physics are so finely tuned that they permit a complex chemistry that, in turn, generates the biological processes that underlie the development of life. It is argued that if these laws were only slightly different—in some instances, infinitesimally so—life, as we understand it, could not have developed.

This is a "coincidence" that modern science has so far found impossible to explain. Needless to say, it is not acceptable to many in the scientific community, largely because of its teleological overtones and its religious implications. Was the universe designed specifically to accommodate intelligent life? (see Gribbin and Rees 1995). This admittedly teleological argument is countered—not too convincingly—by those who insist that a universe capable of sustaining life should not surprise us because the so-called "coincidences" simply describe *our* universe in which life happens to exist.

Unprovable support for the design argument (and one which we will consider in more detail later) is supplied by what might be termed the "multiverse" solution. This hypothesizes that we live in parallel universes. These may take the form of mini or branching universes—an idea that would fit in well with the old steady-state theory of a cosmos that is continuously renewing itself—and in which the laws of physics vary from universe to universe. Or they may take the form of "cosmic bubbles" in which not only are the laws of physics different but they are such as to allow possible alternative scenarios for the same life forms. This is all very interesting as imaginative speculation, but neither advocates nor critics are able to offer a scintilla of evidence.

Nothing that has been said in the foreging discussion has offered an answer to the problem of theodicy. Nor has it really helped with the companion problem of evil. Yet it is surely not entirely unreasonable to suggest that if there is real cogency in the design argument, it at least indicates some kind of providential intelligence that just possibly has our interests at heart.

Should we therefore be prepared to abandon—or, at least, seriously modify—the traditional, purely materialistic view of the universe? Is there more to reality than this? And is it a reality that can be convincingly conceptualized by science? Certainly those who are concerned with the mysteries of the quantum world are not too sure. Neils Bohr said that "Physics is not about how the world *is*, it is about what we can *say* about the world." And another of the founding fathers of quantum physics, Werner Heisenberg, reminded his audience that elementary particles "form a world of potentialities or possibilities rather than one of things or facts" (quoted by Davies and Gribbin 1991, 21). And what are we to make of a reality which is affected by the act of observation, as apparently happens in the quantum world? Yet despite all the uncertainties and the misgivings, there are scientists (for example, Albert Einstein and more recently David Bohm) who think (or hope?) that beneath the seeming disorder there is a kind of order, a coherence that has so far gone undetected.

The quantum world presents us with yet another set of anomalies that some theorists argue may be "solved" by the "parallel-universes" hypothesis, which allows for the possibility of alternative realities. (Interestingly, the mathematics of black holes can indicate an "abandon hope all ye that enter here" scenario *or* the possibility that the intrepid astronaut could be in a tunnel to a parallel universe.) Preposterous as this may sound, it is favored by many quantum cosmologists, even though it implies that there has to be an enormous set of parallel universes with their own spacetimes in order to allow for an equally enormous number of possible outcomes. This would appear to settle the issue of the "coincidences"—those high-precision adjustments—which make intelligent life possible. Because *if* there is an infinite number of universes, each of which represents a different cosmic possibility, then it follows that the question of improbability is neutralized. It would mean that our kind of intelligent life would almost certainly be likely to appear somewhere. (It is rather like the argument that, given the countless planets that must exist in the cosmos, at least one must possess conditions that are conducive to human life.)

Physicists are still struggling to come up with a "theory of everything," which necessarily involves identifying the truly fundamental particles of the universe. They are toying variously with superstring theory, in which the basic entities are not massless points but massless loops or vibrations, and with membrane (M) theory. They are also speculating about a multidimensional universe (currently popular is eleven dimensions instead of four) and with the possibility of a "shadow world" consisting of the usual familiar particles but only interacting with our world through the—as yet—little-understood phenomenon of gravity. These are all extremely conjectural, but every one is, in its own way, an attempt to comprehend the enduring mystery of the cosmos.

So we can say that it is generally accepted that the necessary conditions for the evolution of the organized complexity of the universe are dependent on the remarkable series of coincidences between the values of certain constants. Were these of only slightly different values, then the chain of nuclear reactions that produce carbon—our life form—in the universe would fail to do so. Only the slightest tweak in these values and neither atoms nor stable stars would exist. This teaches us that "if there exists any random element in the initial structure of the universe, or its early evolution . . . then we observe aspects of things that are not typical" (Barrow 1999, 29).

The seemingly bizarre view that there is more "out there" than has previously met the eye, whether it be parallel universes or some other form of multidimensionality, is becoming increasingly accepted among the cosmological community. Theoretical physicists who model the universe mathematically are apparently currently excited to find that the "laws of nature" are becoming simpler and more elegant when expressed in multidimensional (hyperspace) terms. For example, it is argued that although light and gravity appear to obey quite different mathematical "rules," if a fifth dimension is added to the accepted four dimensions of space and time, the equations relating to light and gravity appear to merge (Kaku 1994, ix). It is even suggested that multidimensional conceptualizations may eventually lead to the "theory of everything"—the ultimate goal of physics.

Such ideas may be coherent and compelling, but do they really describe (explain?) the real world(s)? Is everything we know—or think we know—nothing but vibrations in hyperspace? And can space be bent or torn, or even be riddled by a maze of tunnels ("wormholes") to parallel universes, as some cosmologists believe? For those who want to believe in some kind of providential design, such theories suggest a way out of their dilemma. For not only could they provide one possible approach to the problem of theodicy, they also indicate an answer to the oft-publicized eventual "heat-death" of the universe. When, and if, there is such an impending disaster, presumably intelligent life will be able to make its way to an alternative universe. This is, of course, all highly speculative, but we are assured that the accommodating equations do exist. There is no possibility of harnessing the requisite energy to manipulate space-time even in the near future, but maybe we will one day encounter an advanced civilization with the necessary know-how to master hyperspace.

In the meantime we must make do with a somewhat more modest

version of the design argument, and content ourselves with the knowledge that the very existence of humans who can ask questions about the universe presupposes certain physical constraints on the nature of creation: its age, its size, its temperature, and its general chemical composition. Nevertheless, we have to admit that such a version of the anthropic argument is not open to falsification. There is no way in which experimentally it can be shown to be either right or wrong.

And for this reason it has not been well-received by many theoretical physicists. Furthermore, in its parallel-universes form it lends itself to infinite complexity. It can be argued that there are billions of quantum events taking place within every ounce of matter every second. Each event could have thousands of alternative outcomes. Each possible outcome would then be associated with a universe in which that outcome is realized. A multitude of these parallel universes then make up a quantum multiverse which theoretically contains every possible alternative reality.

However, largely due to the work of Stephen Hawking and Sir Martin Rees, there has been something of a revival of the corroborative possibility of parallel universes. It is argued—not unreasonably—that laws in other universes may well be different from those that govern processes in our own universe which have allowed consciousness to develop. Once we have accepted this, those special features "that some theologians once adduced as evidence for providence may be just one element in a cosmic archipelago with each universe starting with its own Big Bang, possibly—so it is surmised—around its own black hole, many of which may have formed when the galaxies were relatively young. Our own universe might be the [planned or unplanned] outcome of such an event in some preceding cosmos. The traditional theological argument from design then reasserts itself in a novel guise" (Rees 1997, 3–4).

There are still, however, all sorts of qualifications that must be made. As we have seen, our own planet is subject to all sorts of catastrophies, seismic disasters, and what are effectively worldwide plagues such as HIV/AIDS. Not least there is the cosmic hazard of some kind of extra-planetary impact that could cause such widespread devastation that life would not recover for decades. Of course, creationists might argue that such contingencies have already been allowed for in the divine economy. But we have to admit that although humanity has been saved so far, the record does not rule out the possibility of such a catastrophic—one might also say, apocalyptic—endgame. The prospect of the complete extinction of human life itself might be justified from one creationist point of view, if the hazard in question is humanity itself. The chances of our species ever reaching another extraterrestrial civilization are extremely remote (unless wormholes in space really do exist), but would we really want to contaminate some hypothetical unsullied alien civilization with the human virus? Is earth's remoteness the result of a cordon sanitaire?

Regardless of these potential eventualities, it still has to be admitted that the universe does appear to be geared towards the possible evolution of intelligent life. We are back then with the anthropic principle. There really are strange "conducive features" that characterize the cosmos as we know it, not least the mysterious force we call gravity—the "bending" of space—which causes the instability that allows stars to form and from which we all derive our existence. Gravity, together with electromagnetism and the strong and weak nuclear forces, are critical to cosmic stability. The numerical values of these basic "constants" (including the masses of elementary particles, their ratios, and the strength of the forces that bind them together) are so fundamental to creation that the universe as we know it could not exist without them. One eminent cosmologist has argued that changes in these subatomic forces are even more constrained than those of gravity, and cannot have changed substantially in several billion years (Rees 1997, 239). Furthermore, the balance within the subatomic world is so fine that if nuclear forces were slightly weaker, no chemical elements other than hydrogen would be stable, and so there would be no nuclear energy to power the stars. On the other hand, if the nuclear forces were slightly stronger than they are relative to electric forces, ordinary hydrogen would not exist, and stars would evolve quite differently (Rees 1999).

The anthropic principle—or some variant of it—has a long lineage and goes back at least as far as the eighteenth-century theologian/mathematician William Paley. As we have noted, it is not supported by many—perhaps most—cosmologists, even though the "coincidences" issue is still something of a puzzle. Hence the appeal of the parallel-universes "solution." This allows the theorist to admit the exceptional nature of our own universe but at the same time to allow that it may not be *so* exceptional that there are not others elsewhere that are curiously like it.

More accommodatingly, we have also seen that the vogue in anthropic reasoning, with its marked teleological implications, comes in different "strengths." In its most robust form it is particularly controversial in that it suggests that the fundamental laws of the universe are such as to permit intelligent observers to exist. Seen in this way, the world becomes a system of shared experience. Indeed, it is even speculated that the cosmos is not just a cold, impersonal "out there" facticity but is actually endowed—somewhat like Fred Hoyle's black cloud—with an impenetrable consciousness.

A quite different view is presented in the work of eminent American physicist Lee Smolin, who attempts to demolish the anthropic principle entirely. Smolin recognizes that for some early (and not so early ?) thinkers, science was tantamount to a search for God, or at least a way of seeking confirmation for the providential design of the universe. Both, he says, are "a search for the absolute, for an understanding of the world that attributes its beauty and order to an eternal and transcendent reality . . . whether the talk is of God, or an eternal and universal law of Nature, the idea that dominates is that the rationality responsible for the coherence we see around us is not in the world, but behind it" (1997, 193–94). He then proceeds to argue that modern science provides us with a means of liberation from this essentially religious worldview. He sees it as far more rational to think of the cosmos with all its coincidences and complexities as a comprehensive, self-organizing system. He is prepared to give some credence to the metaphysical speculation of earlier times but obviously feels that mere mental conjecture with little or no empirical bases is no match for investigative science (2000).

Smolin's view is that there is no reason why the "laws of nature" (insofar as we understand exactly what these are) should not be based upon the principles of natural selection, self-organization, or even "random dynamics." Yet all of these beg many questions, and each needs to be carefully qualified. He admits that these are not simple questions. So there are no simple answers. As he says, they are like asking why there is a world at all. This question can be linked with the yearning for a quasi-religious final explanation, the search for a fundamental theory. It is all part of a "nostalgia for the absolute." Is Smolin's view an antidote for belief in a presiding deity, or is it a substitute for such a belief? But again, what Smolin is apparently not prepared to entertain is the idea that the wish to believe does not invalidate the belief.

We obviously can have no certain knowledge of the world other than that which we actually experience. But is the world as we experience it simply a shadow (as Plato described) of a transcendent reality? Are we to be limited only to the world of the senses? And if we are, can we be sure that the exercise of the accepted physical senses exhausts all that we can know about the world? Presumably if we are prepared to admit this is a possibility we are then in the realm of metaphysics—a realm of real contention that Smolin, for one, is keen to dismiss as unknown and unknowable. On this he may well be right; perhaps we should not confuse science and teleology. But if we keep strictly to science, it would seem that the only really convincing arguments he can offer against the anthropic principle are (a) that it lacks—so far—any predictive capacity (though this may be to confuse a hypothesis with a theory); and (b) that the constants that underpin the principle may not be timeless, a view that is also—so far—unprovable.

The logical outcome of the anti-anthropic point of view is that the universe—somewhat similar in principle to the natural world—is not a product of some mystical process but a product of evolution. (It is worth noting; however, that Darwinian theory does not begin to operate until we have self-replicating cells, and as McFadden reminds us, it would take a totally infeasible tropical-forest-sized yield of complex organic products to make even a single self-replicating molecule.) The universe is seen to have a perfectly rational explanation. It may be "enormously, improbably organized," but this is seen as *self*-organization, and, as such, self-consistent and therefore amenable to rational comprehension. There are no gods; there is no providential ordering of the world, no ultimate point or purpose. In effect, the universe is its own purpose—it exists for itself. Yet no one explains how this principle of self-organization arises or why it exists. In discarding embarrassing teleological implications, there are still unanswered questions. How and why *is* there a process of selection and adaptation? Why replication? Why didn't proto-cells stay proto-cells? And so it goes on. . . . The ultimate mystery remains.

The argument, too, that the universe is ordered so as to produce conscious (i.e., intelligent, self-aware) beings has also met with criticism, even from those who obviously have a certain sympathy with anthropic reasoning, at least in its "weak" form. It is sometimes felt that it is used in the absence of better (i.e., scientific) arguments. But it is conceded that the anthropic argument *could* provide a reason why consciousness is here and need not exist simply because its emergence was favored (necessitated?) by natural selection. But it is doubted if anthropic need or design is the only reason for the evolution of consciousness—something that certainly gives us a *selective* advantage. (For the development of this argument, see Penrose 1999, 127, 561–62.) Yet note that Penrose is a strong advocate of the "independence" of consciousness and does not believe that it is merely a computational mechanism that is soon to be duplicated by machines. Indeed, he argues—à la Pythagoras and Plato—that mathematical concepts/reasoning have a kind of "purity," "a timeless existence independent of our earthly selves."

Roger Penrose's renowned colleague Steven Hawking has also written guardedly about anthropic reasoning. He puts forward the argument that the anthropic principle can be given a precise formulation and is essential when dealing with the question of the origin of the universe. It allows for a large number of possible "histories" of the universe, most of which are not suitable for the development of intelligent life (Hawking 2001, 85–87). The critical question concerns the initial or boundary conditions. What preceded the Big Bang? And was there some kind of predetermination about the nature and direction of the outcome? At this point the Hawking-Penrose equations break down. They indicated a definite beginning to the universe in which the conditions were undoubtedly quite unlike anything known to conventional physics. And they and others have theorized about the phases of the universe's early development. But they are neither prepared to endorse nor repudiate the anthropic principle. Their theoretical escape hatch is the "many histories" idea popularized by the late Richard Feynman (1988).

Regardless of a general consensus among cosmologists, there are still those who have certain reservations or, at least, qualifications about the Big Bang (e.g., Laszlo 1993). An interesting variant is the view that the universe we observe was not created out of a preexisting vacuum but arose as a new cycle within an already existing cosmic background. Was our Big Bang one of a series of singularities, or was it a unique event? It is argued that a universe limited to a single cycle, with a Big Bang issuing from an infinitely small, dense "fireball" to its dispersion in space, could not tune its constants at its own beginning. The idea is intriguing, but does it simply set the problem back one or more stages (cycles)?

So let us remind ourselves of these constants about which there *is* a general consensus. If possible we have to try to explain the consistent orders that we find in the world. Impressionistically, a chance-driven process can only produce divergence. Mere coincidence will not do. A random process may produce atoms, molecules, etc.—

although there is some doubt about this. But how it can produce the fine-tuning for intelligent life seems to be statistically unlikely. This depends on an improbably precise set of values, i.e., the strengths of nature's fundamental forces and the masses of the fundamental particles that appear to have been coordinated from the very beginning (Laszlo 1993):

(1) the expansion rate of the early universe was precise in all directions to an estimated degree of $10^{40}$. This is indicated by the uniformity of the existing cosmic background radiation.

(2) the force of gravity is of such a magnitude that stars can form and exist long enough to generate sufficient energy for life to evolve on suitable planets.

(3) the mass of neutrinos (still somewhat mysterious particles which may have little or no mass and that *may* constitute part of the "dark matter" in the universe), which may have prevented the early universe from collapsing under the force of gravity.

(4) the value of the "strong nuclear force" (i.e., the force that binds the constituents of the atomic nucleus) is such that hydrogen was able to transmute into helium and then into carbon and the other elements indispensible to life as we know it. If this force were only infinitesimally higher, this could not have taken place.

(5) the weak nuclear force is estimated to have the exact value that allows atoms to be expelled in supernovae (exploding stars), so as to provide the basis for the next generation of stars and for the elements that make up the constituents of life.

(6) the weak nuclear force (which affects all matter particles) also has precisely the value, vis-à-vis gravity, which makes hydrogen rather than helium and dominant element in the universe. This allows stars a longer life and therefore favors evolution, as well as contributing—for us, at least—the vital element of water.

It should be pointed out that as far as we know there is no fundamental theory that explicitly predicts that the laws of physics, including these basic physical constants, must be the same in *all* cosmic circumstances. It hardly needs to be reiterated that physicists are only on the mere fringes of discovery. Perhaps, too, it would be as well to remember John Wheeler's cautionary view that even if one day they come up with the "theory of everything," they will still be disappointed. They will still face the unanswerable problem of why nature obeys (has to obey?) this set of equations.

The anthropic principle has also spawned the hypothesis that our universe is really a cosmic experiment—perhaps one among many—

initiated by superior beings for reasons we have yet to fathom (see the work of Edward Harrison, 1991). The alternative is that the universe could be the creation of *a* supreme being. Or it is possible to amalgamate both ideas by combining the supreme being with other lesser though superior intelligences who together are responsible for creation (a view that doesn't foreclose further scientific enquiry). It all sounds rather far-fetched, but hardly more far-fetched than a universe that appears from nothing. The Big Bang theory may well be true, but—viewed dispassionately—it is quite bizarre. Whence this infinitely small "fireball" or vacuum energy that spontaneously burst into matter? How does it come to possess universe-forming potential? What caused it to change from its initial state? What determined the nature and direction of that change? Again, there are just too many unanswered questions, and one has to ask, what is the most reasonable/plausible hypothesis?

On the basis of the evidence we have, the Special Creation hypothesis has to be regarded as untenable. Given the precarious situation of the Earth in space and its continued vulnerability to all kinds of disasters, both actual and potential, it takes an act of blind, uncomprehending credulity to believe that our planet was set up for our habitation. On the other hand, to believe that the cosmos and the very "seeds of life" have a designer label is not so irrational. This does not solve the problem of theodicy, but it does go some way to providing some assurance that despite the perplexities, life has an ultimate purpose.

Life of various kinds is almost certainly to be found elsewhere in the universe (and maybe in other universes too, if cosmological speculation is anything to go by). It so happens that here it has evolved its peculiar forms as a function of its environment. These—paradoxically—are both wonderful and terrible, shaped, as they are, by the struggle for status and natural resources. It could even be that the potentiality for life arrived (à la Hoyle, Crick, et al.) from outer space and that Earth is not our natural—or eventual—dwelling place. Does this mean that having come from the stars we may eventually return to the stars? The great religions hint at this, some more specifically than others. Indeed, the idea of the Kingdom of Heaven, which may be an anticipatory rather than immanent concept, may not be as far-out as it sounds, and the "Incarnation" may be a providential exercise in damage limitation. How else is humanity to be saved from itself?

So the problem remains. I, for one, still do not understand—perhaps cannot expect to understand. Whatever the variety of claims of various religious systems, none has a convincing cosmology; none has a verifiable instance of divine revelation or intervention. All claims must be taken on faith. And many are partial and self-contradictory, though some undoubtedly provide more persuasive evidence than others.

All religions are marred by histories of misunderstanding, hypocrisy, and cruelty, though some have generated exceptional instances of courage and self-sacrifice. This is how we are—as far as we know, the most wonderful and most terrible creatures in the cosmos. For me, the ambiguity of the human situation is exemplified in the true account of a mass killing by German SS Einsatzgruppen in Russia (as recounted by Gerald Reitlinger, 1956), which was observed by an undetected laborer working in the area. He said that just before the shooting he noticed that one man was holding a small, uncomprehending child. With only seconds to live, what can you do? How can you explain? The observer recalled that the man appeared to speak softly to the child and then pointed to the sky.

# Bibliography

Ablin, D., and M. Hood. 1987. *The Cambodian Army*. New York: Sharpe.

Adams, M. M. 1999. *Horrendous Evils and the Goodness of God*. Ithaca: Cornell.

Aggleton, P. 1992. *AIDS: Rights, Risk and Reason*. London: Falmer Press.

Altizer, T. 1967. *The Gospel of Christian Atheism*. London: Collins.

Anders, T. 1994. *The Evolution of Evil*. Chicago: Open Court.

Andrew, C., and D. Gordievsky. 1990. *KGB: The Inside Story*. London: Hodder & Stoughton.

Arrian, 1971. *The Campaigns of Alexander* Trans. Aubrey de Selincourt. New York: Dorset Press.

Ayer, A. J. 1946. *Language, Truth and Logic*. Rev. ed. London: Gollanz.

Barber, N. 1973. *Lords of the Golden Horn*. London: Macmillan.

Barlow, D. 1979. *Sexually Transmitted Diseases: The Facts*. Oxford: Oxford University Press.

Barnett, C. 1978. *Bonaparte*. London: Allen & Unwin.

Barrow, J. 1999. *Between Inner Space and Outer Space*. Oxford: Oxford University Press.

Barrow, J., and F. Tipler. 1986. *The Anthropic Cosmological Principle*. Oxford: Oxford University Press.

Berger, P. 1969. *The Social Reality of Religion*. London: Faber & Faber.

Bohm, D. 1980. *Wholeness and the Implicate Order*. London: Routledge, Kegan and Paul.

Bolt, B. 1988. *Earthquakes*. New York: Freeman.

Bosworth, A. 1988. *Conquest and Empire*. Cambridge Mass.: Cambridge University Press.

Bourke, J. 2001. *The Second World War: A People's History*. Oxford: Oxford University Press.

Brooke-Shepherd, G. 1998. *Ironmaze*. London: Pan Books.

Brown, C. 1969. *Philosophy and Christian Faith*. London: Tyndale Press.

Buren, P. van. 1963. *The Secular Meaning of the Gospel*. London: Student Christian Movement.

Burn, A. 1973. *Alexander the Great and the Middle East*. Harmondsworth: Penguin.

Burtt, E. 1957. *Man Seeks the Divine*. New York: Harper & Row.

Caesar, J. 1951. *The Conquest of Gaul*. Trans. S. Handford. Harmondsworth: Penguin.

Cairns-Smith, A. 1985. *Seven Clues to the Origins of Life*. Cambridge, Mass.: Cambridge University Press.

173

Carlton, E. 1990. *War and Ideology.* London: Routledge.

———. 1992. *Occupation: The Policies and Practices of Military Conquerors.* London: Routledge.

———. 1995. *Values and the Social Sciences.* London: Duckworth.

———. 2000. *The Paranormal: Research and the Quest for Meaning.* Aldershot, England: Ashgate.

———. 2001. *Militarism: Rule without Law.* Aldershot, England; Ashgate.

Cartwright, F., and M. Biddis. 1991. *Disease and History.* New York: Dorset Press.

Castleden, R. 1998. *Atlantis Destroyed.* London: Routledge.

Chardin, T. de. 1951. *The Phenomenon of Man.* New York: Harper Brothers.

Chown, M. 2001. *The Universe Next Door.* London: Headline Books.

Coates, J. 1949. *The Crisis of the Human Person.* London: Longmans Green.

Cobb, J. B. 1981. *Encountering Evil: Live Options in Theodicy.* Ed. Steven T. Davis. Louisville: Westminster John Knox Press.

Coles, P., ed. 1999. *The New Cosmology.* Cambridge, England: Icon Books.

Conquest, R. 1990. *The Great Terror: A Reassessment.* London: Hutchinson.

Crankshaw, E. 2000. *In the Shadow of the Winter Palace.* New York: De Capo Press.

Crawford, D. 1978. *The Roman Republic.* London: Fontana.

Crick, F. 1981. *Life Itself: Its Origins and Nature.* New York: Simon & Schuster.

Davies, P. 1987. *The Cosmic Blueprint.* London: Heineman.

———. 1994. *The Last Three Minutes: Conjectures about the Ultimate Fate of the Universe.* New York: Basic Books.

———. 1998. *Quantum Revolution.* London: Flamingo Books.

Davies, P., and J. Gribben. 1991. *The Matter Myth.* London: Viking Books.

Davis, S., ed. 1981. *Encountering Evil: Live Options in Theodicy.* Louisville, Ky: Westminster John Knox Press.

Dawkins, R. 1976. *The Selfish Gene.* Oxford: Oxford University Press.

Delsemme, A. 2000. *Our Cosmic Origins.* Cambridge: Cambridge University Press.

Dixon, B. 1996. *Power Unseen: How Microbes Rule the World.* Oxford: W. H. Freeman.

Driver, H., ed. 1964. *America on the Eve of Discovery.* Englewood Cliffs, NJ: Prentice-Hall.

Duve, C. de. 1995. *Vital Dust.* New York: Basic Books.

Dwyer, J. 1989. *The Body at War.* London: Unwin Hyman.

Dyson, F. 1979. *Disturbing the Universe.* New York: Harper & Row.

Edwards, R. 1972. *Reason and Religion.* New York: Harcourt, Brace & Javanovich.

Eigen, M. 1992. *Steps Towards Life.* Oxford: Oxford University Press.

Elliot, G. 1973. *Twentieth Century Book of the Dead.* Harmondsworth: Penguin.

Evans, G. 1982. *Augustine on Evil.* Cambridge, Mass.: Cambridge University Press.

Ewing, A. 1968. *Non-Linguistic Philosophy.* London: Allen & Unwin.

Feynman, R. 1988. *QED: The Strange Theory of Light and Matter.* Princeton: Princeton University Press.

Flew, A., and A. Macintyre. 1955. *New Essays in Philosophical Theology*. London: Student Christian Movement.

Francis, P., and S. Self. 1983. The Eruption of Krakatau. *Scientific American* (Nov.): 172–87.

Fromm, E. 1964. *The Heart of Man*. New York: Harper & Row.

Gabel, C. 1964. *Man Before History*. Englewood Cliffs, NJ: Prentice-Hall.

Gardiner, P. 1961. *The Nature of Historical Explanation*. Oxford: Oxford University Press.

Gellner, E. 1957. Is Belief Really Necessary?. *Hibbert Journal.*

———. 1964. *Thought and Change*. London: Weidenfeld & Nicholson.

———. 1992. *Postmodernism, Reason and Religion*. London: Routledge.

Gerth, H., and C. Wright Mills, ed. 1957. *Alexander the Great*. London: Weidenfeld & Nicholson.

Greene, B. 2000. *The Elegant Universe*. London: Vintage Books.

Greenwood, D., and W. Stini. 1977. *Nature, Culture and Human History: A Biocultural Introduction to Anthropology*. New York: Harper & Row.

Gregory, A. Psychical Research as a Social Activity. *Journal of the Society of Psychical Research* 51:1981.

Gribben, J., and M. Rees. 1995. *The Stuff of the Universe*. London: Penguin.

Griffin, D. R. 1991. *Evil Revisited: Responses and Reconsiderations*. Albany, NY: Albany State University Press.

Hargrove, B. 1979. *The Sociology of Religion*. Arlington Heights: AMH Publishing.

Harper, A. 1990. *The Theodicy of Suffering*. New York: Edwin Mellen Press.

Harrison, E. 1991. *The Science of the Universe*. Cambridge, Mass.: Cambridge University Press.

Hastings, M. 1981. *Das Reich*. London: Michael Joseph.

———. 1987. *The Korean War*. London: Michael Joseph.

———. 2000. *Bomber Command*. London: Pan.

Hawking, S. 2001. *The Universe in a Nutshell*. London: Bantam Books.

Hazen, R. 1997. *Why Aren't Black Holes Black?* New York: Anchor Books.

Hebblethwaite, B. 1976. *Evil, Suffering and Religion*. London: Sheldon Press.

Hemmings, J. 1974. *The Conquest of the Incas*. London: Macmillan.

Herzstein, R. 1982. *When Nazi Dreams Came True*. London: Abacus.

Hick, J. 1974. *Faith and Knowledge*. 2nd ed. London: Fontana.

———. 1977. *The Myth of God Incarnate*. London: Student Christian Movement.

Hodges, H. 1979. *God Beyond Knowledge*. London: Macmillan.

Hohne, H. 1969. *The Order of the Death's Head*. London: Pan.

Horne, J., and A. Kramer. 2001. *German Atrocities, in 1914: A History of Denial*. London: Yale University Press.

Horsman, R. 1969. *The War of 1812*. London: Eyre & Spottiswoode.

Hospers, J. 1961. *Human Conduct*. New York: Harcourt, Brace, & World.

Hourani, A. 1991. *A History of the Arab Peoples*. London: Faber & Faber.

Hoyle, F. 1983. *The Intelligent Universe*. London: Michael Joseph.

Innes, H. 1970. *The Conquistadors*. London: Thames & Hudson.

Joad, C. E. M. 1932. *Philosophical Aspects of Modern Science*. London: Allen & Unwin.

————. 1942. *God and Evil*. London: Faber and Faber.

————. 1951. *The Recovery of Belief*. London: Faber & Faber.

Johnson, P. 1985. *A History of the Modern World*. London: Weidenfeld & Nicholson.

Jouvenal, B. de Power. 1948. Trans. J. Huntington. London: Hutchinson.

Kaku, M. 1994. *Hyperspace*. Oxford: Oxford University Press.

Kamil, J. 1996. *The Ancient Egyptians*. Cairo: The American University of Cairo Press.

Karlen, A. 1995. *Plague's Progress, a Social History of Man and Disease*. London: Gollancz.

Karnow, S. 1983. *Vietnam: A History*. Harmondsworth: Penguin.

Katz, F. 2000. *The Ancient American Civilisations*. London: Phoenix Press.

Kauffman, S. 1993. *The Origins of Order*. Oxford: Oxford University Press.

Keaveney, A. 1982. *Sulla, The Last Republican*. Beckenham, England: Croom Helm.

Kohn, G. 1998. *Encyclopedia of Plague and Pestilence*. Ware, England: Wordsworth.

Kuper, L. 1981. *Genocide*. Harmondsworth: Penguin.

Larrimore, M., ed. 2001. *The Problem of Evil: A Reader*. Oxford: Blackwell.

Laszlo, E. 1993. *The Creative Cosmos*. Edinburgh: Floris Books.

Lenin, V. 1969. *Selected Works*. London: Lawrence & Wishart.

Levy, R. 1971. *The Structure of Islam*. Cambridge, Mass.: Cambridge University Press.

Lewis, C. S. 1954. *The Problem of Pain*. London: Bles.

Mackie, J. 1971. Evil and Omnipotence. In *The Philosophy of Religion*, ed. Basil Mitchell. Oxford: Oxford University Press.

Manchester, W. 1969. *The Arms of Krupp*. London: Michael Joseph.

Mavrodes, G. 1970. *The Rationality of Belief in God*. Englewood Cliffs, N.J.: Prentice-Hall.

McCabe, H. 2000. God, Evil and Divine Responsibility. *Philosophy of Religion, A Guide and Anthology*, ed. Brian Davies. Oxford: Oxford University Press.

McFadden, J. 2000. *Quantum Evolution*. London: Flamingo Books.

McNeil, W. 1976. *Plagues and Peoples*. Harmondsworth: Penguin.

Meadow, M., and R. Kahoe. 1984. *Psychology of Religion*. New York: Harper & Row.

Miles, R. 1959. *Religion and the Scientific Outlook*. London: Allen & Unwin.

Mitchell, B. 1971. *The Philosophy of Religion*. Oxford: Oxford University Press.

Monod, J. 1972. *Chance and Necessity*. London: Collins.

Muir, R. 1996. *Britain and the Defeat of Napoleon*. New Haven: Yale University Press.

Nicholson, N. 1985. *Napoleon: 1812*. London: Weidenfeld & Nicholson.

Niemeyer, G. 1966. *Outline of Communism*. London: Ampersand.

Nikiforuk, A. 1991. *The Fourth Horseman*. London: Fourth Estate.

O'Brien, J. 1992. *Alexander the Great*. London: Routledge.

O'Dea, T. 1970. *Sociology and the Study of Religion*. New York: Basic Books.

Oldenbourg, Z. 1961. *Massacre at Monsegur*. London: Weidenfeld & Nicholson.

————. 1966. *The Crusades*. New York: Random House.

Ormsby, E. L. 1984. *Theodicy in Islamic Thought, the Dispute over al-Ghazali, Best of All Possible Worlds*. Princeton: Princeton University Press.

Payne, R. 1994. *The Crusades*. London: Robert Hale.

Penrose, R. 1999. *The Emperor's New Mind*. Oxford: Oxford University Press.

Peterson, F. 1972. *The Common Philosophy*. New York: The Philosophical Library.

Phillips, D. Z. 1971. Religious Beliefs and Language Games. In *The Philosophy of Religion*, ed. Basil Mitchell. Oxford: Oxford University Press.

———. 1993a. The Problem of Evil. In *Reason and Religion*, ed. Stuart Brown. London: Macmillan.

———. 1993b. *Wittgenstein and Religion*. London: Macmillan.

Pilger, J. 1989. *Heroes*. London: Pan.

———. 1992. *Distant Voices*. London: Vintage Books.

Polkinghorne, J. 1989. *Science and Providence: God's Interaction with the World*. London: Society for the Promotion of Christian Knowledge.

Popper, K. 1966. *The Open Society and Its Enemies*, vols. 1 and 2. London: RKP.

Prosche, H. 1966. *The Genesis of Twentieth Century Philosophy*. London: Allen & Unwin.

Rees, M. 1997. *Before the Beginning*. London: Simon & Schuster.

———. 1999. *Just Six Numbers*. London: Weidenfeld & Nicholson.

Reichenbach, B. R. 1982. *Evil and a Good God*. New York: Fordham University Press.

Reitlinger, G. 1956. *The SS, The Alibi of a Nation*. London: Heinemann.

Richardson, A. 1966. *Religion in Contemporary Debate*. London: Student Christian Movement Press.

Robinson, J. 1963. *Honest to God*. London: Student Christian Movement Press.

Robinson, W. 1946. *The Devil and God*. London: Student Christian Movement Press.

Rowe, W. L. 1979. The Problem of Evil and Some Varieties of Atheism, American *Philosophical Quarterly* 16:335–41.

Runciman, W. 1989. *A Treatise on Social Theory*, vol. 2, Cambridge, Mass.: Cambridge University Press.

Russell, B. 1948. *A History of Western Philosophy*. London: Allen & Unwin.

Schutze, A. 1978. *The Enigma of Evil*. Trans., from German, Eva Lauterbach. Edinburgh: Floris.

Shapiro, R. 1986. *Origins: A Skeptic's Guide to the Creation of Life on Earth*. New York: Summit Books.

Short, P. 1999. *Mao: A Life*. London: Hodder Stoughton.

Shukman, H. 1999. *Stalin*. Stroud, England: Sutton Publishing.

Simkin, T., and L. Siebert. 1994. *Volcanoes of the World*. Washington, D.C.: Smithsonian.

Smolin, L. 1997. *The Life of the Cosmos*. London: Weidenfeld & Nicolson.

———. 2000. *Three Roads to Quantum Gravity*. London: Weidenfeld & Nicolson.

Spence, J. 1999. *Mao*. London: Weidenfeld & Nicolson.

Stanesby, D. 1985. *Science, Reason and Religion*. Beckenham: Croom Helm.

Surin, K. 1986. *Theology and the Problem of Evil*. Oxford: Blackwell.

Swinburne, R. 1986. *Providence and the Problem of Evil.* Oxford: Blackwell.

Thomas, K. 1971. *Religion and the Decline of Magic.* London: Weidenfeld & Nicolson.

Thorne, K. 1994. *Black Holes and Time Warps, Einstein's Outrageous Legacy.* London: Picador.

Tilley, T. 1991. *The Evils of Theodicy.* Washington, D.C.: Georgetown University Press.

Tomlin, E. 1986. *Philosophers of East and West.* London: Oak Tree Books.

Toynbee, Sir A. 1970. *A Study of History.* Oxford: Oxford University Press.

Trigg, R. 1975. *Reason and Commitment.* Cambridge, Mass.: Cambridge University Press.

———. 1980. *Reality and Risk.* Brighton, England: Harvester.

Wallace, A. 1966. *Religion: An Anthropological View.* New York: Random House.

Weber, M. 1922. *The Sociology of Religion.* London: Methuen, 1966.

Weinberg, G. 1994. *The World at Arms.* Cambridge, Mass.: Cambridge University Press.

Weinberg, S. 1988. *The First Three Minutes: A Modern View of the Origin of the Universe.* New York: Basic Books.

Wilkins, R. 1994. *Deadly Diseases.* London: Robert Hale.

Williams, C. 1966. *Adaptation and Natural Selection: A Critique of Some Current Evolutionary Thought.* Princeton: Princeton University Press.

Williams, G. 1996. *Plan and Purpose in Nature.* London: Weidenfeld & Nicholson.

Wilson, E. O. 1975. *Sociobiology: The New Synthesis.* Cambridge: Harvard University Press.

Witney, B. 1998. *Theodicy: An Annotated Bibliography of the Problems of Evil, 1960–1991.* Virginia: Garland Philosophy Documentation Centre.

Wolfe, L. 1958. *In Flanders Fields.* London: Longmans.

Worsley, R. 1996. *Human Freedom and the Logic of Evil.* Basingstoke, England: Macmillan.

Yinger, J. M. 1957. *Religion, Society and the Individual.* New York: Macmillan.

Zebrowski, E. 1988. *Earthquakes.* New York: Freeman.

———. 1997. *Perils of a Restless Planet.* Cambridge, Mass.: Cambridge University Press.

Ziegler, P. 1970. *The Black Death.* Harmondsworth: Penguin.

# Index